Backroad Bicycling in Wisconsin

Backroad Bicycling in Wisconsin

Second Edition

JANE E. HALL AND
SCOTT D. HALL

28 Scenic Tours
through Lakes,
Forests, and
Glacier-Carved
Countryside

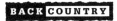 Backcountry Guides
Woodstock, Vermont

An invitation to the reader

Although it is unlikely that the roads you cycle on these tours will change much with time, some road signs, landmarks, and other items may. If you find that such changes have occurred on these routes, please let the author and publisher know, so that corrections may be made in future editions. Other comments and suggestions are also welcome. Address all correspondence to: Editor, Backroad Bicycling Series, Backcountry Guides, P.O. Box 748, Woodstock, VT 05091

Library of Congress Cataloging-in-Publication Data
Hall, Jane E.
    Backroad bicycling in Wisconsin : 28 scenic tours through lakes, forests, and glacier-carved countryside / Jane E. Hall and Scott D. Hall.—2nd ed.
        p.   cm.
    Rev. ed. of: 30 bicycle tours in Wisconsin. C1994.
    ISBN 088150548X
    1. Bicycle touring—Wisconsin—Guidebooks. 2. Wisconsin—Guidebooks. I. Hall, Scott D. II. Hall, Jane E. 30 bicycle tours in Wisconsin. III. Title.
GV1045.5.W6H35 2003
796.6'4'09775—dc21

                                                                    2002043731

Second Edition
Previously published as *30 Bicycle Tours in Wisconsin*

Quotation on page 17 from *Travels with Charley* by John Steinbeck, copyright © 1961, 1962 by The Curtis Publishing Co.; © 1962 by John Steinbeck; renewed © 1990 by Elaine Steinbeck, Thom Steinbeck, and John Steinbeck IV. Used by permission of Viking Penguin, a division of Penguin Books USA Inc.

Cover and interior design by Bodenweber Design
Cover photo © Dennis Coello
Interior photographs by the authors
Maps by Moore Creative Designs, © 2003 The Countryman Press

Published by Backcountry Guides, a division of The Countryman Press, P.O. Box 748, Woodstock, VT 05091

Distributed by W.W. Norton & Company, Inc., 500 Fifth Avenue, New York, NY 10110

Printed in the United States of America

10 9 8 7 6 5 4 3 2

To our parents:
Mary, Ed, Pat, Doug, and Bob
for instilling a love of the outdoors
and encouraging our spirit of exploration.

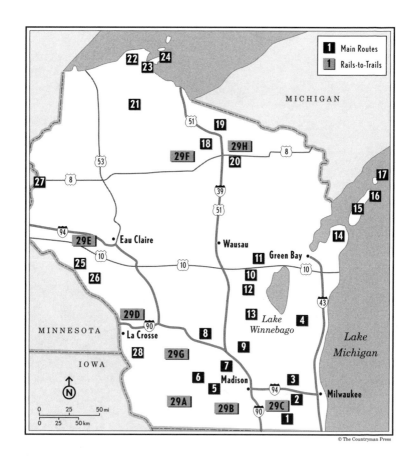

MICHIGAN

MINNESOTA

IOWA

Lake Winnebago

Lake Michigan

Eau Claire

Wausau

Green Bay

La Crosse

Madison

Milwaukee

Main Routes

Rails-to-Trails

N

0   25   50 mi
0   25   50 km

© The Countryman Press

CONTENTS

PREFACE TO THE SECOND EDITION   Our revision of this book was prompted by a move back to the Midwest after five years living in Central America and New York City. As we rediscovered our favorite bicycling routes, we found that some things have changed. New parks, inns, restaurants, and galleries have opened up. There are now more than 30 off-road bicycle trails, many on former railroad lines. New roads have been added and old roads improved. What remains the same is Wisconsin's wonderfully varied landscape and its welcoming attitude toward two-wheeled travelers. We hope you will find this second edition useful as you travel down some of the best back roads anywhere.

BACKROAD BICYCLE TOURS AT A GLANCE

RIDE	REGION	STARTING POINT
1. Southern Kettle Moraine State Forest	Southeastern Wisconsin	Ottawa Lake State Park
2. Dousman/Waterville	Southeastern Wisconsin	Dousman
3. Holy Hill	Southeastern Wisconsin	Delafield
4. Northern Kettle Moraine State Forest	Southeastern Wisconsin	Plymouth
5. Blue Mounds	Southwestern Wisconsin	Blue Mound State Park
6. Spring Green/ Wisconsin River/ Frank Lloyd Wright Country	Southwestern Wisconsin	Tower Hill State Park
7. Devil's Lake/Baraboo Hills	Southwestern Wisconsin	Devil's Lake State Park
8. Wisconsin Dells/ Aldo Leopold Country	Southwestern Wisconsin	Mirror Lake State Park
9. Pardeeville/Amish Country	Southwestern Wisconsin	Pardeeville
10. Waupaca Chain of Lakes	Central Wisconsin	Hartman Creek State Park
11. Waupaca/Scandinavia/Iola	Central Wisconsin	Waupaca
12. Wild Rose/ Christmas Tree Country	Central Wisconsin	Wild Rose

DISTANCE	TERRAIN	HIGHLIGHTS
31.1 miles	Rolling	Kettle Moraine Scenic Drive; Ottawa Lake State Park; Old World Wisconsin
9.7 or 25.7 miles	Rolling	Old Military Road; Pabst Farms; Kettle Moraine Scenic Drive
13.1 or 41.7 miles	Rolling to hilly	Holy Hill Cathedral; Kettle Moraine Scenic Drive; Historic Monches
33.4 miles	Rolling to hilly	Kettle Moraine Scenic Drive; Ice Age Visitor Center; Elkhart Lake
34.5 miles	Rolling to hilly	Blue Mound State Park; Hidden Valleys; Little Norway Historic Site; Military Ridge State Trail
22.5 or 31.4 miles	Rolling to hilly	Tower Hill State Park; Spring Green; Global View bazaar; Taliesin
29.5 miles	Rolling to hilly	Devil's Lake State Park; Circus World Museum; Historic Baraboo
24.2 miles	Rolling	Mirror Lake State Park; Wisconsin Dells; International Crane Foundation
27.4 or 47.7 miles	Rolling	Rolling wooded countryside; Amish craftsmen
23.8 miles	Gently rolling	Hartman Creek State Park; Historic Rural; Chain of Lakes
21.7 or 31.7 miles	Gently rolling	Historic Waupaca; Iola Old Car Show grounds; rolling wooded countryside
31.8 miles	Gently rolling	Historic Wild Rose; Mount Morris Park and Vista; abundant wildlife

RIDE	REGION	STARTING POINT
13. Green Lake/ White River Marsh/ Princeton	Central Wisconsin	Green Lake
14. Southern Door County	Door County	Sturgeon Bay
15. Ephraim/Baileys Harbor Peninsula State Park	Door County	Ephraim
16. Ellison Bay/Gills Rock/ Newport State Park	Door County	Ellison Bay
17. Washington Island	Door County	Gills Rock
18. Lac du Flambeau	Northern Wisconsin	Lac du Flambeau
19. Boulder Junction/ Manitowish Waters	Northern Wisconsin	Boulder Junction
20. Rhinelander	Northern Wisconsin	Rhinelander
21. Chequamegon National Forest	Northern Wisconsin	Cable
22. Bayfield/Cornucopia/ Washburn	Bayfield Peninsula	Bayfield
23. Bayfield Orchards	Bayfield Peninsula	Bayfield

DISTANCE	TERRAIN	HIGHLIGHTS
6 or 35.7 miles	Gently rolling	Green Lake; White River Marsh; Princeton Flea Market; Lawsonia Estate
42.1 miles	Flat to gently rolling	Sturgeon Bay; Potawatomi State Park; Lake Michigan Vistas
11.9 or 38.2 miles	Gently rolling	Picturesque Ephraim; Cana Island Lighthouse; Peninsula State Park; Sunset Bike Trail; art galleries
19.2 miles	Flat to gently rolling	Lake Michigan Vistas; Newport State Park; Gills Rock—Tip of Peninsula; art galleries
24.3 miles	Flat to rolling	Washington Island Ferry; Icelandic Settlement; art galleries; Schoolhouse Beach
20.4 or 34.2 miles	Flat to gently rolling	Deep North Woods; Indian Cultural Center; casino
33.9 or 46.8 miles	Gently rolling to rolling	Deep North Woods; cranberry bogs; Big Lake swimming area; Crystal Lake Bike Trail
14 or 26.8 miles	Flat to gently rolling	Lumberjack Museum; North Woods and lakes; Wisconsin River vistas
24.5 or 38.7 miles	Rolling to hilly	Chequamegon National Forest; Lake Owen; Lake Namekagon; artisans
54.7 miles	Rolling	Historic Bayfield; Washburn; Apostle Islands National Lakeshore; artisans
10.6 or 32.7 miles	Rolling to Hilly	Historic Bayfield; Apple and Cherry Orchards; Little Sand Bay; Apostle Islands Vistas

RIDE	REGION	STARTING POINT
24. Madeline Island	Bayfield Peninsula	Bayfield
25. Lake Pepin/Stockholm/ Great River Road	Western Wisconsin	Stockholm
26. Alma/Great River Road	Western Wisconsin	Alma
27. St. Croix Falls/ Interstate State Park	Western Wisconsin	St. Croix Falls
28. Westby/Avalanche/ Hidden Valleys	Western Wisconsin	Westby
29. Favorite Railroad-Bed Trails		
A. Military Ridge Trail	Southwest Wisconsin	Verona
B. Sugar River Trail	Southwest Wisconsin	New Glarus
C. Glacier Drumlin Trail	Southeast Wisconsin	Cottage Grove
D. Great River Trail	Western Wisconsin	Trempealeau
E. Red Cedar Trail	Western Wisconsin	Menomonie
F. Bearskin Trail	Northern Wisconsin	Minocqua
G. Elroy-Sparta Trail	Western Wisconsin	Elroy or Sparta
H. Crystal Lake Trail	Northern Wisconsin	Boulder Junction

DISTANCE	TERRAIN	HIGHLIGHTS
18.9 or 31.7 miles	Flat	Madeline Island Ferry; Big Bay State Park; Madeline Island Maritime Museum; Apostle Islands Vistas
25.3 or 40.4 miles	Rolling to Hilly	Stockholm Artisans; Lake Pepin Vistas; Little House in the Big Woods; Coulee Country
31.4 or 43.7 miles	Gently Rolling to Hilly	Buena Vista Park; Coulee Country; Upper Mississippi Wildlife Refuge
33.6 miles	Rolling to Hilly	Interstate State Park; Historic Osceola; Dalles of the St. Croix River; Gandy Dancer Trail
16.9 or 31 miles	Rolling to Hilly	Hidden Valleys; Amish Farmlands; Avalanche Weavers; Cheese Factories
14.2 miles	Flat	Riley; Sugar River Watershed
32 miles	Flat	New Glarus Swiss Heritage; Scenic Sugar River
31.4 miles	Flat	Aztalan Historic Site; wildlife refuge
17 miles	Flat	Trempealeau; Mississippi River vistas; Perrot State Park
15 miles	Flat	Red Cedar River; Downsville; The Creamery Restaurant
20 miles	Flat	Minocqua; North Woods and lakes
32 miles	Flat	Hidden Valleys; railway tunnels
22 miles	Flat to gently rolling	Northern Highlands State Forest; swimming beaches

INTRODUCTION

We moved quickly northward, heading for Wisconsin...a
noble land of good fields and magnificent trees, a gentleman's
countryside, neat and white-fenced...I had never been to
Wisconsin, but all my life I had heard about it, and eaten its
cheeses, some of them as good as any in the world. And I
must have seen pictures. Everyone must have. Why then was
I unprepared for the beauty of the region, for its variety of
field and hill, forest and lake?

—John Steinbeck, *Travels with Charley, In Search of America*

GEOGRAPHY Wisconsin's shape resembles a mitten—a fitting
symbol since its inhabitants are often snowbound from November
to March. The state measures about 450 miles from the most
northerly to the most southerly point and approximately 250
miles east to west. The thumb of the mitten is the popular Door
County peninsula, surrounded by the waters of Lake Michigan
and Green Bay. This narrow strip of land, with its abundant
orchards, artist galleries, and working lighthouses, is one of the
state's most popular cycling areas.

The tip of the mitten extends icy fingers into Lake Superior,
the largest and most mysterious of the Great Lakes and the second largest inland body of water in the world. The northern
third—above the knuckles—is blanketed by state and national
forest land, where tall pines and pristine lakes lure hunters and

anglers, as well as cyclists. In the palm sits rich, rolling farmland dotted with red barns, Lake Wobegon–like towns, and winding farm-to-market roads. Along the western border lies the mighty Mississippi River, where high bluffs and hidden valleys challenge even the mountain-bred bicyclist.

There are few rides in this book where you won't come in contact with some body of water. With more than 15,000 sparkling inland lakes, there's always one nearby for a refreshing plunge or impromptu lakeside picnic. The state borders on 860 miles of Great Lakes shoreline and boasts 190 miles of Mississippi River frontage. Hundreds of square miles of marsh and wetlands are resting places for migratory birds and home to myriad other creatures. Most famous of these is Horicon Marsh, where more than 200,000 Canada geese stop annually in October for a brief respite en route to their wintering grounds.

GEOLOGY Much of Wisconsin's landscape is a gift of the glaciers. When the last major ice mass covering the continent disappeared about 10,000 years ago, it so transformed the state that it is referred to as the Wisconsin Glacier. During the melting process, the glacier sprinkled its burden of unsorted boulders, rocks, and sand across the state. This glacial till, or drift, covers approximately two-thirds of Wisconsin, accounting for the state's fertile soil and gently rolling terrain. The most prominent glacial features are seen in the northern and southern units of the Kettle Moraine forest in southeastern Wisconsin.

In sharp contrast is Wisconsin's southwest corner, which stands untempered by glacial ice. Referred to as the driftless area, this part of the state is characterized by steep hills and narrow winding valleys, reminiscent of Vermont. The Door County peninsula also escaped glaciation. Its solid limestone bedrock, an extension of the Niagara escarpment, separated the advancing ice mass into two distinct paths or lobes that now make up the waters of Green Bay and Lake Michigan.

EARLY HISTORY Wisconsin's original inhabitants were comprised of eight major Native American tribes—the Winnebago, Menominee,

Chippewa, Potawatomi, Fox, Sauk, and Dakota. The culture remains strong today, and several of this book's rides pass through reservation land, where customs are preserved through festivals and powwows. Other routes pass by impressive tribal burial mounds.

The first European to reach the area was Frenchman Jean Nicolet, who landed on the shores of Green Bay in 1634, dressed in a Mandarin robe and convinced he had finally found the elusive passage to the Orient. He was welcomed as a god by the Winnebago tribe, and while disappointed not to find the wealth and spices of China, he was impressed with the land's abundance of fish, fur, and timber.

Next came the fur traders, who were given rights to their bounty as an incentive for colonizing what had become known as New France. Trading posts were established in 1669 at La Pointe, on Madeline Island in Lake Superior, and at Green Bay, at the base of the Door County peninsula. Each party of fur traders was accompanied by several Jesuit missionaries, many of whom were explorers in their own right, including Father Jacques Marquette, who along with Louis Joliet discovered the Mississippi River in 1673.

ETHNIC HERITAGE A look at the Wisconsin map reveals a proud European heritage. Rhinelander, New Berlin, New Lisbon, Pulaski, Scandinavia, Rome, Hollandale, Germantown, Brussels, and Luxemburg are only a few of many Wisconsin towns settled during the nineteenth century's massive migration from Europe to the western Great Lakes states.

Lumber and mining industries recruited heavily in the Scandinavian countries, accounting for the predominance of Norwegian and Swedish surnames in Wisconsin today. Eventually saving enough to purchase small farms, Scandinavian settlers built the state's agricultural base. It was the Danes who introduced large-scale dairy farming to Wisconsin. Icelandic immigrants brought fishing expertise to the turbulent waters around Washington Island, which remains the country's largest Icelandic settlement. The Germans came with an aptitude for grain farming and a thirst for beer. Milwaukee soon became a brewing center dominated by immigrants named Pabst and Schlitz.

Leading a new wave of immigration are the Hmong, refugees from Laos who were resettled in the Midwest following the Vietnam conflict. Wisconsin is home to about 45,000 Hmong, who live primarily in the communities of Green Bay, Appleton, Wausau, and Eau Claire. With their agrarian background, the Hmong have excelled at farming. Look for Hmong farmers selling fresh herbs and produce at local farmer's markets. Some Hmong farmers have devoted themselves to cultivating ginseng, a lucrative crop grown in the Wausau area.

ROAD SYSTEM Thanks to a prosperous dairy industry and the need to get milk to market daily, Wisconsin is laced with an extensive network of smoothly paved secondary roads, most with little traffic other than a sputtering tractor or stray Holstein. State and national forest roads in the northern part of the state offer both paved and unpaved options through unspoiled wilderness. Wisconsin has a bicycle-friendly reputation, and motorists generally give cyclists a welcoming wave and a wide berth.

Wisconsin roads are well cared for, though harsh winter weather necessitates continuous maintenance. Road repairs and detours are frequent during the summer season. Occasionally major highways are detoured onto smaller county roads, resulting in more traffic than usual. A listing of major highway construction projects is available from the state Department of Transportation and can be useful in predicting such detours. The Wisconsin State Legislature has mandated that 5-foot shoulders be added to all state highways carrying more than 1,000 cars and 25 cyclists per day. The improved shoulders are being added as these roads require resurfacing. The road labeling system in Wisconsin is simple, and most intersections are well-marked. State highways in Wisconsin are designated with one- or two-digit numbers; county highways are designated with single, double, or triple letters; and town roads are given descriptive names. Nearly any county or town road, chosen at random, will be suitable for cycling. State highways are appropriate only for short distances, except where paved shoulders have been added. The state has also designated a number of Wisconsin's most scenic roads as Rustic Roads. To qualify, these roads must exhibit "rugged terrain, native vegetation, native wildlife, or open areas with agricultural vistas." The Rustic Road must also be "lightly traveled and not scheduled for improvements which would change its rustic characteristics." Speed limits are restricted to 45 miles per hour, and roads are marked with a brown and yellow sign. (See *Resources.*) Wisconsin is a leader in the national movement to turn abandoned railroad beds into bicycle trails. Completed in 1965, the state's Elroy-Sparta trail was one of the first rails-to-trails conversions in the country. The state has now developed more than 30 such trails. The flat terrain (no more than 3 percent grade) and absence of vehicle traffic make the trails ideal for families with children, beginning bicyclists, and those looking for a leisurely ride. The trail surface is a finely screened limestone that is suitable for hybrid and mountain bikes. Touring bikes should be equipped with 1⅛- or 1¼-inch tires. A daily or yearly trail pass must be purchased to use the trails. In addition to railroad-bed trails, numerous communities have developed off-road bicycle trails and paths, many of which are paved. A sampler of our favorite trail rides is included in this book; see chapter 29.

WEATHER AND SEASONS The cycling season in Wisconsin generally runs from early May through late October. The occasional warm, sunny day in April or November is relished. The spring cyclist gets a jump on the tourist traffic, a head start on summer fitness plans and the season's special rewards—a trillium blossom peeking out along a wooded roadside or a fawn scampering across the road. Farm fields are a patchwork panorama of green in every shade, and the air smells of fertile, freshly tilled soil. Daytime temperatures average 55 to 75 degrees, with occasional rain showers.

June, July, and August are prime cycling months, with daytime temperatures ranging in the 70s, 80s, and occasionally 90s, often with high humidity. These are great months to take advantage of Wisconsin's many clear swimming lakes and to indulge in its creamy, rich ice cream. In the summer you will happen upon small town festivals, auctions, flea markets, and band concerts. Bratwurst and sweet corn are always available for an impromptu lunch.

Autumn is both the most beautiful and most fleeting of seasons for cycling in Wisconsin. Labor Day leaves the bugs and tourists behind, and small towns take on an added charm as they return to a slower, post-season pace. Roadside stands overflow with fresh produce at harvest time, and you can spin your wheels to a serenade of southbound geese overhead.

The color calendar in Wisconsin spans from mid-September in the northern third of the state to a mid-October peak in the southern third. The leaves change later on the Bayfield and Door County peninsulas because of the warming effect of surrounding water. Daytime temperatures range from 55 to 70 degrees in September and 45 to 60 degrees in October.

SELECTING YOUR BIKE A properly fitted and tuned bicycle is the key to a positive cycling experience. The rides described here are best enjoyed on either a touring bike or a hybrid bike. Though all of the rides are on paved roads, a mountain bike would also be appropriate for the shorter tours.

A touring bike looks like a racing bike but has a longer frame, allowing you to stretch out and distribute your weight across the entire frame and both wheels. This provides stability if carrying panniers and camping equipment on longer tours. Touring bikes generally have dropped (ram's horn) handlebars, which allow you a choice of hand positions and let you keep a low profile when riding against a strong wind. We recommend that a touring bike be equipped with 1⅛- or 1¼-inch tires—these will see you through the occasional gravel stretch or cavernous pothole.

The hybrid, or cross-bicycle, combines the comfort and durability of a mountain bike with the lighter weight and riding ease of a touring bike. The hybrid is usually equipped with upright handlebars and gear levers on or below the handlebar grips. With gear levers readily accessible, it's possible to shift without moving your hands. This can also be a drawback, as the lack of variations in hand position can result in sore hands, arms, and shoulders. Handlebar extensions, available as an optional accessory for most hybrids, help alleviate this problem.

Many people prefer the upright riding position because it provides a full view of the scenery, without straining the neck or back. However, it's important to note that a higher profile translates into more wind resistance. Hybrids are generally equipped with 1⅜-inch tires, adequate for any road surface, including rough gravel.

While Wisconsin is not a mountainous state, most people are surprised at the hilliness of the terrain. Whether you choose a touring bicycle or hybrid bicycle, we recommend that you select a bike with a triple chain ring. The triple chain ring will be found on a bike with 18 or 21 gears. You'll find that the smallest of the three chain rings (also called the granny gear) is a lifesaver when climbing the short steep hills of the Kettle Moraine State Forest or the bluffs along the Mississippi River.

OTHER EQUIPMENT   Here are a few other items that will make your ride safer and more enjoyable.

A helmet is your most important piece of bicycling equipment. It has been proven repeatedly that helmets greatly reduce the risk of a fatal head injury resulting from a fall or collision. Many people mistakenly believe that if they are experienced riders, they do not need to wear a helmet. Another fallacy is that helmets need not be worn when cycling close to home or on off-road trails. The fact is that most accidents are not related to rider ability, but are "freak" occurrences that can't be predicted or controlled.

The good news is that helmets are becoming lighter and more comfortable every year. An up-to-date helmet consists of a punctureproof plastic shell, a protective Styrofoam liner, and a strong strap and buckle. When you purchase a helmet, look for a label that says it meets American National Standards Institute (ANSI) or Snell Memorial Foundation safety standards. A helmet must fit well and be adjusted properly to be effective. It should rest evenly on your head above your eyebrows (some have a tendency to tilt back), and the straps should be secure. A good test is to open your mouth wide—if the helmet is properly adjusted you should feel a slight pressure on top of your head.

A good pair of sunglasses not only protects your eyes from the sun but from flying insects, dirt, and other airborne debris. If you look at the windshield of your auto in the summer, you will understand why glasses are important.

Padded cycling gloves will help alleviate sore palms, elbows, and shoulders. They will also cushion your hands in a fall.

A rearview mirror prevents you from looking over your shoulder for traffic, which causes you to veer out into the road. Mirrors are available in many styles. Some models fit onto your brake hoods or handlebars; others attach to your helmet.

A handlebar bag is handy for carrying a camera, wallet, rain gear, snacks, and other incidental items. Most come with a transparent vinyl map case on top. This is a convenient way to carry your directions or map.

Bicycle computers record your mileage for a day trip, along with your average speed and the total distance covered over a longer journey. Because this book gives you the cumulative mileage for each turn and point of interest, a computer makes it easier to follow the written directions. One caution though—don't focus on your computer or you'll miss the passing scenery.

A pump, a spare inner tube, a patch kit, and a few basic tools are essential if your ride takes you out in the country, away from bicycle shops and gas stations. Be sure that your pump is compatible with the valve on the type of inner tube you use; there are two types—Schrader and Presta. A basic tool kit should include an Allen wrench set, tire levers, chain tool, adjustable wrench, Phillips screwdriver, and regular screwdriver.

A bicycle lock is important if you plan to stop for any length of time.

A first-aid kit that includes basic supplies such as Band-Aids, gauze bandages, antiseptic, aspirin, and sunscreen is good insurance. Make up your own kit and keep it in your handlebar bag at all times, replenishing items as needed.

While no special clothing is required for cycling, there are a few items you may want to consider for reasons of comfort. Nearly every touring cyclist ends up riding in the rain at some time or another. Adequate rain gear makes cycling in wet weather bearable and, in many cases, even enjoyable. Raincoats consist of two types, breathable and nonbreathable. Breathable rainwear, made of brand-name fabrics such as Gore-Tex, is preferable since it keeps the rain out and also lets your perspiration escape. Less expensive vinyl raincoats will do the job if you ride only periodically. Ponchos are usually not suitable for cycling since they tear easily and tend to act as a sail in high winds.

Saddle soreness is a common problem for beginning cyclists and can be alleviated somewhat by using a gel bicycle saddle and/or by wearing padded cycling shorts. Cycling jerseys or other shirts made from fabrics with moisture-wicking properties will keep you dry and comfortable during very warm or very cool weather.

Weather in Wisconsin often changes quickly. Always bring an extra layer of clothing along, just in case. Mornings can be quite cool, especially in the spring and fall. If you are planning a trip during the spring or fall, include tights or narrow warm-up pants, full-fingered gloves, and a headband or cap that can be worn under your helmet. Cyclists who experience soreness in the feet or ankles may choose to wear cycling shoes, which have an extra-firm sole. They are also narrower than other athletic shoes and fit more easily into toe clips. Many cyclists are now choosing shoes with cleats that snap into the pedal itself. This kind of system increases pedaling efficiency but is not without risks. It takes some practice to get used to inserting and removing shoes from the pedals when starting and stopping.

BICYCLE SAFETY   While bicycling is a fun and relaxing activity, it is important to be alert and attentive at all times. The following safety guidelines are worth reviewing periodically, even if you are an experienced cyclist.

Riding in control   Never ride at a speed faster than is comfortable for you. On downhill stretches, keep your weight to the back of the saddle and pump your brakes to prevent overheating. Watch for sand or loose gravel, especially on corners. This is especially important in the spring months in Wisconsin, when sand deposited by snowplows during the winter remains on the road.

Obstacles Anticipate obstacles by looking well ahead of your bicycle. Scan the road for rough spots, debris, potholes, glass, and other items. Always check the traffic behind you, using your rearview mirror, before steering around these areas. Place your wheels perpendicular to railroad tracks and drainage grates.

Riding single file Wisconsin state law requires that cyclists ride single file. Allow an ample distance between your bike and those ahead of you. When stopping to rest or chat, stay well off the road.

Hand and spoken signals Let motorists and other cyclists know of your intention to turn, change lanes, pass, or stop by using hand and spoken warnings. It is customary to say "car up" and "car back" to warn people around you of oncoming traffic.

Dogs Expect to come across dogs in Wisconsin's rural farm areas. If you are chased by a dog, remain calm, stop pedaling, and dismount your bicycle. Place the bicycle between you and the dog. Point at the animal and shout "stay" or "go home" in a commanding voice. Once the dog has quieted and retreated, walk slowly away without turning your back to it. Never attempt to outpedal a dog or to spray water or repellent from a moving bicycle. These actions are likely to cause a fall or to aggravate the dog into attacking cyclists riding with you.

Loose clothing Watch out for loose clothing that can catch in moving parts. Shoelaces that wrap around pedals are particularly hazardous—they should be double-tied and tucked into your shoes.

Severe weather Thunderstorms and tornadoes are common during Wisconsin's hot and humid summer weather. If you see severe weather approaching, or if you hear weather-warning sirens, seek shelter immediately. Don't hesitate to ask if you can wait out the storm in someone's barn or garage if you are in a remote area.

Slippery pavement Brakes don't function well on wet roads that may be covered with a slippery layer of grease and oil. Test your brakes frequently for effectiveness and pump them lightly and continually, well in advance of your planned stop. In the fall, wet leaves can make road surfaces treacherous.

Food and water Always carry a water bottle and some light snacks with you. A second water bottle is advisable if you're biking in an area with few services. Camelback manufactures a system that allows you to drink without removing your hands from the handlebars. Water is carried in a backpacklike reservoir and the cyclist drinks from a tube much like drinking through a straw. You will maintain a higher energy level if you eat small amounts throughout the day and drink regularly, beginning well before you become thirsty. If you find yourself losing steam, specially formulated energy drinks such as Gatorade and snacks such as Cliff Bars or Powerbars can provide a needed boost.

HOW TO CHOOSE THE RIGHT TRIP FOR YOU When deciding

which tour to embark on, you should consider both the distance and terrain. Remember that a 20-mile ride in hilly terrain may be more demanding than a 35-mile ride on level terrain. A strong wind also leads to faster fatigue and should be factored into your decision about how far to go.

A beginning rider or someone who exercises only occasionally will probably find a 20- to 25-mile ride quite satisfying. Novices may also find it useful to join organized tour groups that offer the "safety net" of tour leaders and a support van until they gain more confidence and endurance. An intermediate cyclist or a person who engages in aerobic exercise regularly will comfortably ride 30 to 40 miles a day, with enough time for lunch and sight-seeing/shopping stops. While advanced cyclists frequently ride 50, 75, or even 100 miles in a day, these distances are goals to work up to gradually. Keeping a mileage log is a good way to track your progress throughout the season and to better determine your ability level.

USING THE DIRECTIONS AND MAPS When using this book, we

suggest that you read the descriptive information about each tour first. This will give you a feel for the area and help you decide if the scenery and attractions are of interest to you. Then, look at the map for a general "lay of the land."

A condensed version of the directional cues is also included on each map.

Mileages may vary slightly depending on variations in calibrations of computers, whether or not you ride in a straight line (most of us don't), and how often you take detours or wrong turns. Occasionally road signs become twisted or become dorm-room souvenirs. If what you see doesn't jibe with your internal compass, ask the first person you meet for directions. You will get back on course quickly and probably have a pleasant conversation, too.

Most computers can be switched off temporarily when you detour off the route and restarted when you return to the route. For tours that begin at Wisconsin state parks, mileage is calculated from the ranger station. Mileage for tours beginning at smaller parks is calculated from the park exit.

If you want to add to, or improvise on, the rides presented in this book, you may wish to carry a detailed map of the area in which you are cycling. Other map sources are listed in Resources.

Contact the local chambers of commerce for a complete list of lodging and dining options. The ones mentioned in the rides have special qualities, and we would recommend them to a friend.

RESOURCES   **Wisconsin State Bike Maps**   The Bicycle Federation of Wisconsin sells a set of four, large fold-out maps that classifies all state and county roads in terms of conditions for bicycling and identifies recreational bicycle trails. The maps are available for sale at many Wisconsin bike shops or by calling 1-800-362-4537. The cost is $3.95 for individual maps (the state is divided into quadrants) or $12.95 for the complete set of four maps.

Wisconsin Biking Guide   This 72-page booklet describes and maps out a selection of Wisconsin's best on-road tours, mountain bike tours, and tours on bike trails. It also lists major bicycle events and rides that take place in Wisconsin. The publication is free from the Wisconsin Department of Tourism, P.O. Box 7976, Madison, WI 53707-7976 or by calling 1-800-432-8747.

Wisconsin's Rustic Roads...   This 64-page booklet provides maps and descriptions of the state's 90 designated Rustic Roads. These roads were selected for their exceptional scenic and historic interest. For a free copy call 1-800-432-8747 or 608-266-8108.

The Wisconsin Atlas and Gazetteer   This comprehensive atlas provides a detailed rendering of national, state, county, and town roads, as well as topographical information. It is of special value to the cyclist because it indicates which roads are paved and which are not. Contact DeLorme Mapping, P.O. Box 298, Yarmouth, ME 04096, 207-846-7000.

Wisconsin County Maps Maps of Wisconsin's 72 counties are available from the Wisconsin Department of Transportation, Document Sales Office, 3617 Pierstorff Street, Madison, WI 53707, 608-246-3265, or by contacting the county clerk at the courthouse in an individual county.

Milwaukee Map Service, Inc. This company puts out a very detailed set of maps dividing the state into four quadrants—northeast, northwest, southeast, and southwest. Contact Milwaukee Map Service, Inc., 959 N. Mayfair Road, Milwaukee, WI 53226, 1-800-525-3822.

SOUTHEASTERN
WISCONSIN

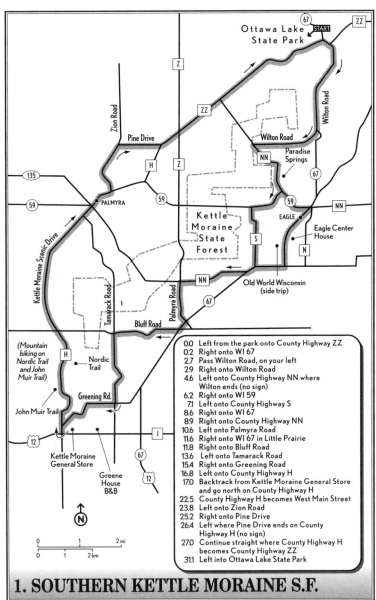

Ottawa Lake State Park

START

Kettle Moraine State Forest

PALMYRA

EAGLE

Eagle Center House

Old World Wisconsin (side trip)

Zion Road

Pine Drive

Wilton Road

Paradise Springs

Kettle Moraine Scenic Drive

Tamarack Road

Palmyra Road

Bluff Road

(Mountain biking on Nordic Trail and John Muir Trail)

Nordic Trail

Greening Rd.

John Muir Trail

Kettle Moraine General Store

Greene House B&B

0.0	Left from the park onto County Highway ZZ
0.2	Right onto WI 67
2.7	Pass Wilton Road, on your left
2.9	Right onto Wilton Road
4.6	Left onto County Highway NN where Wilton ends (no sign)
6.2	Right onto WI 59
7.1	Left onto County Highway S
8.6	Right onto WI 67
8.9	Right onto County Highway NN
10.6	Left onto Palmyra Road
11.6	Right onto WI 67 in Little Prairie
11.8	Right onto Bluff Road
13.6	Left onto Tamarack Road
15.4	Right onto Greening Road
16.8	Left onto County Highway H
17.0	Backtrack from Kettle Moraine General Store and go north on County Highway H
22.5	County Highway H becomes West Main Street
23.8	Left onto Zion Road
25.2	Right onto Pine Drive
26.4	Left where Pine Drive ends on County Highway H (no sign)
27.0	Continue straight where County Highway H becomes County Highway ZZ
31.1	Left into Ottawa Lake State Park

0	1	2 mi
0	1	2 km

N

1. SOUTHERN KETTLE MORAINE S.F.

Southern Kettle Moraine State Forest

- **DISTANCE:** 31.1 miles
- **TERRAIN:** Rolling

Ice Age glaciers created the gentle undulations of the Kettle Moraine countryside, where you're nearly always climbing the ridge of an esker or coasting down a kame. In the springtime, the wooded roadsides are decorated with the soft pastels of columbines and pasqueflowers; later in the season, the color is intense and fiery as the hardwoods put on their autumn finery.

The forest is interspersed with fertile farmland and vast marshy areas. Springs that once drew visitors from around the world to "take the waters" at Waukesha County's fashionable health spas now trickle unattended into secluded trout streams.

Nearly all of this tour takes place within the boundaries of the state forest; acorn-shaped markers along the road point out portions of the popular Kettle Moraine Scenic Drive. If you ride a mountain bike, you might wish to combine this route with some off-road cycling at one of several popular mountain bike trails along the way. Directions are given if you wish to visit Old World Wisconsin, one of the country's premier outdoor living museums, while on the tour. Set out early if you plan to do this—it takes a minimum of four hours to tour the entire complex.

The tour begins at Ottawa Lake State Park. From I-94, take WI 67 south for about 15 miles to County Highway ZZ. Turn right onto County Highway ZZ, following signs to the park. Good picnic facilities, a swimming beach, rest rooms, and water are available.

0.0 Left from the park onto County Highway ZZ.

0.2 Right onto WI 67.
This is a busy road, but it has a good shoulder.

1.5 McClintock Springs Children's Fishing Area.

1.9 Wayside with water.

2.7 Pass Wilton Road, on your left.

2.9 Right onto Wilton Road.

4.6 Left onto County Highway NN where Wilton ends (no sign).

5.8 Paradise Springs Nature Area is to your left, opposite the log cabin.
This is a catch-and-release trout fishing area. Ages 16 to 64 need a trout stamp, available from the Department of Natural Resources; the season is January 1 to September 30. There is also a well-designed nature trail that illustrates how two types of stream vegetation, veronica and elodea, shelter smaller trout and provide food for insects eaten by fish.

Expect lots of ups and downs in this glacier-carved countryside.

The property was originally owned by Louis J. Petit, owner of Morton Salt Company. The clear pool of water known as Paradise Springs is 4 feet deep, 47 degrees in temperature, and pumps out 30,000 gallons of water per hour. The springs are formed when rainwater and melting snow seep into hills and ridges and build up an underground water table that is higher in elevation than the water table in the surrounding lowlands. Water from the elevated water table follows sand and gravel layers and seeps from the hill as a spring. There is a fieldstone springhouse built by Petit in the 1930s, which originally had a wooden dome roof.

Photos show the area when it was a resort and popular honeymoon spot. In later years, a bottling plant for spring water, a horse track, and golf course were located on the property. Across the road is the hand-hewn Gotten Cabin, built by a Prussian immigrant in the 1850s.

Turn left from Paradise Springs, continuing on County Highway NN.

6.2 Right onto WI 59.
At this point, it's possible to make a side trip to Old World Wisconsin. See directions below.

7.1 Left onto County Highway S.

7.9 Kettle Moraine Ranch offers horseback riding.

8.6 Right onto WI 67.

8.9 Right onto County Highway NN.

10.6 Left onto Palmyra Road where County Highway NN ends.
County Highway Z goes right and Little Prairie Road goes straight here.

11.6 Right onto WI 67 in Little Prairie.

11.8 Right onto Bluff Road.

13.6 Left onto Tamarack Road.

15.4 Right onto Greening Road.

16.8 Left onto County Highway H.

17.0 The Kettle Moraine General Store. Backtrack from store and go north on County Highway H.
This is a friendly store featuring health foods and natural beauty aids, run by Mike Bettinger, an avid bicyclist and bike advocate. Cyclists gravitate toward the smoothies and a sandwich called the "Mexican Smile." Mike can also provide a map of mountain bike trails in the Kettle Moraine forest and give you an update on trail conditions. If you've discovered a squeaky brake or forgotten a needed accessory, the Backyard Bike Shop on the premises will gladly assist you.

The Greene House Bed & Breakfast (262-495-8771) serves hearty home-cooked meals and has a gigantic "guitar gallery" featuring vintage instruments. It is located east of the General Store on WI 12.

To continue, backtrack from the store and head north on County Highway H.

18.6 The John Muir and Nordic Trails are popular for mountain biking and cross-country skiing.
There are rest rooms here.

20.1 Bald Mountain Lookout and Nature Trail is on your right.

22.5 County Highway H becomes West Main Street as you enter Palmyra.

22.7 Palmyra Village Park is to your right.

23.0 Downtown Palmyra (all two blocks of it) has several small cafés and an ice cream parlor.

23.8 Left onto Zion Road.

25.2 Right onto Pine Drive.

26.4 Left where Pine Drive ends on County Highway H (no sign).

27.0 Continue straight on County Highway ZZ here.
County Highway H becomes County Highway ZZ, where County Highway Z intersects.

31.1 Left into Ottawa Lake State Park.

OLD WORLD WISCONSIN SIDE TRIP   Turn left onto WI 59 and follow it into the town of Eagle, then turn right onto WI 67. You'll pass the Eagle Centre House (262-363-4700), a circa-1846 stagecoach inn that offers bed-and-breakfast lodging. Follow WI 67 south to the Old World Wisconsin entrance. Use caution on WI 59 and WI 67; both are busy roads.

This 560-acre outdoor living museum consists of about 50 historic buildings constructed by Wisconsin's immigrant settlers. The buildings have been moved from their original locations throughout Wisconsin and carefully reassembled at the Old World complex. Clusters of buildings represent 10 ethnic farmsteads and an 1870s crossroads village. Norwegian, Danish, Finnish, Polish, and German areas are included. Authentically costumed staff go about their daily chores—preparing meals, tending barns and livestock, and sowing and cultivating crops. Special events mark the changing of seasons. The Clausing Barn Restaurant serves cafeteria-style food with an ethnic twist.

To rejoin the route, turn right onto WI 67 at the exit and continue to County Highway NN. Refer to the 8.9-mile mark for the remaining directions. The detour will add about 2 miles to your total mileage.

Bicycle Repair Service

Bicycle Doctor, Main Street, Dousman; 262-965-4144

Backyard Bike and Ski Shop (at the La Grange General Store), WI 12 and County Highway H, La Grange; 262-495-8600

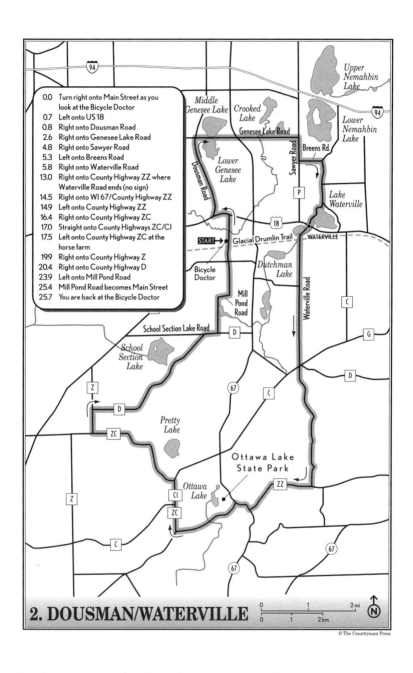

0.0	Turn right onto Main Street as you look at the Bicycle Doctor
0.7	Left onto US 18
0.8	Right onto Dousman Road
2.6	Right onto Genesee Lake Road
4.8	Right onto Sawyer Road
5.3	Left onto Breens Road
5.8	Right onto Waterville Road
13.0	Right onto County Highway ZZ where Waterville Road ends (no sign)
14.5	Right onto WI 67/County Highway ZZ
14.9	Left onto County Highway ZZ
16.4	Right onto County Highway ZC
17.0	Straight onto County Highways ZC/CI
17.5	Left onto County Highway ZC at the horse farm
19.9	Right onto County Highway Z
20.4	Right onto County Highway D
23.9	Left onto Mill Pond Road
25.4	Mill Pond Road becomes Main Street
25.7	You are back at the Bicycle Doctor

2. DOUSMAN/WATERVILLE

© The Countryman Press

Dousman/Waterville

- **DISTANCE:** 9.7 or 25.7 miles
- **TERRAIN:** Rolling

With its rolling hills, meticulously kept farms, and stacked stone fences, stretches of this ride may remind you of Kentucky. Horses have always played a part in area history. A century ago, as many as 400 stagecoach teams passed through nearby Summit Centre each day on the old military road between Milwaukee and Madison. A wealthy Waterville family built a track where young men raced and bet on their horses. Today, as you cycle through this area you'll see thoroughbreds grazing peacefully in green pastures and pass recreational horseback riders out on trail rides from local stables.

This area has long been known for its rich farmland, most notably the Pabst Farms owned by Fred Pabst of the Pabst Brewing Company. While his brother Gustav served as president of the Milwaukee-based brewing company, Fred had no interest in that aspect of the business and preferred a quiet rural life. He began by raising horses and eventually developed a world famous Holstein herd. The production of milk and cheese saw the brewing family through the lean years of Prohibition. Contrary to popular belief, Fred's farm did not supply grain for the Pabst brewery, though it did supply the smaller local breweries.

The family's 1,500-acre farm, located at the junction of Interstate Highway 94 and WI 67, has long been the largest piece of farmland in southeastern Wisconsin. The past decade has seen changes in the landscape, including the development of an industrial park on this land. Currently, plans are under way for a controversial new project to create a "planned community" on the former Pabst property. Blueprints call for business and residential areas, as well as open space, within the community.

This tour passes through Dousman, a thriving small town that was formerly a stop on the Chicago and Northwestern Railroad. The town was nicknamed Bullfrog Station because of moonlight serenades coming from surrounding bogs and marshes in the summer months. Tradition lives on at Dousman Derby Days, an annual summer celebration, which includes a parade, live entertainment, and a frog-jumping contest. Look for a change in terrain as you pedal through the historic crossroads village of Waterville. The path of the Wisconsin Glacier is evident as you alternately pedal and coast through a series of kettles on the Kettle Moraine Scenic Drive.

The tracks that once brought railroad passengers to Dousman now bring bicyclists. The former railroad bed has been converted into the Glacial Drumlin Trail, a 53-mile trail that connects Waukesha and Cottage Grove. The shorter option on this tour returns on the trail. The trail also provides a good warm-up ride or an alternate ride for members of your group who prefer flatter terrain.

This tour begins in downtown Dousman in front of the Bicycle Doctor, adjacent to the trailhead for the Glacial Drumlin Trail. Here you will find rest rooms, water, and plenty of parking. The Bicycle Doctor is a bike shop and then some. Always dream of wearing the yellow jersey? In addition to bikes, accessories, and expert repair services, this shop has an espresso bar where you can sip coffee and watch Tour de France videos. Bagels, energy bars, smoothies, and trail passes are also available here.

To get to the start of the tour, take I-94 from the east or west to WI 67. Exit south on WI 67 and continue until you reach US 18. Turn right on US 18 and follow the signs to Dousman. Turn left onto Main Street, which will take you into downtown. The Bicycle Doctor is on your right.

Thoroughbreds graze peacefully at one of the area's many horse farms.

0.0 Turn right onto Main Street as you look at the Bicycle Doctor and follow it through downtown.

0.7 Left onto US 18 where Main Street ends.
This is a busy road with a good shoulder.

0.8 Right onto Dousman Road (keep right, heading north).

2.6 Right onto Genesee Lake Road and follow through the narrow isthmus between Upper and Lower Genesee Lakes.

2.7 Boat landing parking area has rest rooms.

3.4 Cross WI 67 and continue on Genesee Lake Road.

4.8 Right onto Sawyer Road.

5.3 Left onto Breens Road.

5.8 Right onto Waterville Road.

7.3 Cross US 18 and continue on Waterville Road.

Waterville Road is a Rustic Road and part of the Kettle Moraine Scenic Drive. This junction was a hub of activity in the mid-1800s when a new road (present-day US 18) was built to connect Milwaukee and Madison. An old stone general store stood here until 1992, when it was moved to the living museum at Old World Wisconsin.

7.7 Cross the Glacial Drumlin Trail.
Shorter Option: *If you turn right onto the trail here, it is about 2 miles back to Dousman.*

10.2 Cross County Highway G and continue straight on Waterville Road. *Waterville Road becomes hilly as you enter the Kettle Moraine State Forest. You will pass a number of turnoffs for picnic areas and campgrounds, all of which have rest rooms.*

13.0 Right onto County Highway ZZ where Waterville Road ends (no sign).

13.1 Ottawa Trails Horse Park (rest rooms and water).

14.2 Scuppernong Trails Picnic Area.

14.5 Right onto WI 67/County Highway ZZ for a short distance.

14.9 Left onto County Highway ZZ.
Ottawa Lake State Park. There are picnic shelters, rest rooms, water, a campground, and a nice swimming beach here.

16.4 Right onto County Highway ZC.

17.0 Straight onto County Highways ZC/CI.

17.5 Left onto County Highway ZC at the horse farm.
This is a shady, pleasant ride.

19.9 Right onto County Highway Z.

20.4 Right onto County Highway D.

23.9 Left onto Mill Pond Road. Careful, this is an easy turn to miss.

25.4 Mill Pond Road becomes Main Street as you enter Dousman.

25.7 Dousman City Park has rest rooms, water, and a picnic shelter.

25.7 You are back at the Bicycle Doctor.

Bicycle Repair Service

The Bicycle Doctor, Main Street (next to the Glacial Drumlin Bicycle Trail), Dousman; 262-965-4144

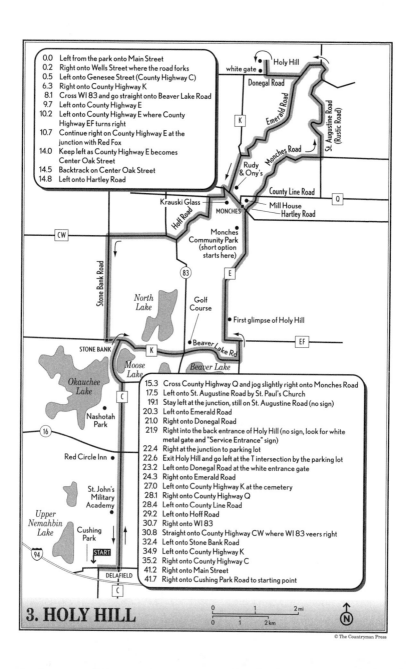

0.0	Left from the park onto Main Street
0.2	Right onto Wells Street where the road forks
0.5	Left onto Genesee Street (County Highway C)
6.3	Right onto County Highway K
8.1	Cross WI 83 and go straight onto Beaver Lake Road
9.7	Left onto County Highway E
10.2	Left onto County Highway E where County Highway EF turns right
10.7	Continue right on County Highway E at the junction with Red Fox
14.0	Keep left as County Highway E becomes Center Oak Street
14.5	Backtrack on Center Oak Street
14.8	Left onto Hartley Road

Holy Hill
white gate
Donegal Road
Emerald Road
St. Augustine Road (Rustic Road)
K
Monches Road
Rudy & Ony's
County Line Road
Q
Krauski Glass
Hoff Road
MONCHES
Mill House
Hartley Road
Monches Community Park (short option starts here)
CW
83
E
Stone Bank Road
North Lake
Golf Course
First glimpse of Holy Hill
STONE BANK
K
Beaver Lake Rd
EF
Moose Lake
Beaver Lake
Okauchee Lake
C
Nashotah Park
16
Red Circle Inn
St. John's Military Academy
Upper Nemahbin Lake
Cushing Park
START
94
DELAFIELD
C

15.3	Cross County Highway Q and jog slightly right onto Monches Road
17.5	Left onto St. Augustine Road by St. Paul's Church
19.1	Stay left at the junction, still on St. Augustine Road (no sign)
20.3	Left onto Emerald Road
21.0	Right onto Donegal Road
21.9	Right into the back entrance of Holy Hill (no sign, look for white metal gate and "Service Entrance" sign)
22.4	Right at the junction to parking lot
22.6	Exit Holy Hill and go left at the T intersection by the parking lot
23.2	Left onto Donegal Road at the white entrance gate
24.3	Right onto Emerald Road
27.0	Left onto County Highway K at the cemetery
28.1	Right onto County Highway Q
28.4	Left onto County Line Road
29.2	Left onto Hoff Road
30.7	Right onto WI 83
30.8	Straight onto County Highway CW where WI 83 veers right
32.4	Left onto Stone Bank Road
34.9	Left onto County Highway K
35.2	Right onto County Highway C
41.2	Right onto Main Street
41.7	Right onto Cushing Park Road to starting point

3. HOLY HILL

0	1	2 mi
0	1	2 km

N

Holy Hill

- **DISTANCE:** 41.7 miles (13.1 miles for the shorter option from Monches)
- **TERRAIN:** Rolling to hilly

The Gothic spires of the cathedral at Holy Hill reign supreme over the surrounding glacial countryside, reminiscent of a European castle. Holy Hill is a religious shrine that each year draws thousands of pilgrims in search of the healing powers that cured a French hermit. In the autumn, people make a pilgrimage of another kind, to enjoy the breathtaking display of colored oaks and maples. Located halfway between Milwaukee and Madison, this area is growing rapidly but still offers some pleasant back roads riding past prime fishing lakes and century-old country estates.

To reach the start, take I-94 to County Highway C North, which becomes Genesee Street as you enter the village of Delafield. Turn left onto Main Street at the first stop sign and continue to Cushing Park Road (opposite the Mason Creek Winery). Turn right into this pleasant little park along the river, which has rest rooms, picnic tables, and parking. The shorter option for this tour begins at the Community Park in the village of Monches. If you choose the shorter option, take I-94 to WI 83 North. Follow WI 83 to the village of North Lake. Turn right onto County Highway VV. Turn left onto County Highway E and follow it to Monches. The Community Park is on the left just before the village. Go immediately to 13.9 miles for the directions.

The cathedral at Holy Hill

0.0 Left from the park onto Main Street.

0.2 Right onto Wells Street where the road forks.

0.4 Hawks Inn (262-646-2140) is to your right.
Built of hand-hewn timbers and handmade nails, the inn was built by Nelson Page Hawks, one of Delafield's founders, as a stagecoach stop on the Milwaukee to Madison plank road. Guided tours are available May through October.

0.5 Left onto Genesee Street (County Highway C) through downtown Delafield.
The Steeple Shops and Town Hall Shops both house antiques vendors.

0.9 St. John's Northwestern Military Academy is to your left.
Delafield is well known for this military prep school for boys, founded in 1884 by Sydney Smythe, a student at nearby Nashotah House Episcopal Seminary. The school's charter stresses quality, self-discipline, team spirit, and leadership. Enter the gates and take a spin through the campus to view the Old Gothic–style stone buildings with fortress like towers, battlements, and serrated roofs. Especially beautiful is the Church of St. John Chrysostom, built in 1851.

3.3 To your left at the junction with Watertown Plank Road is one of southern Wisconsin's finest restaurants, the Red Circle Inn.

Watertown Plank Road was one of many such roads, also called corduroy roads, built in Wisconsin in the mid-1800s. It was used by fur traders and farmers hauling products to Milwaukee and supplies back over this route. Since timber was plentiful, plank roads were relatively cheap to construct, durable, practical, and safe. Built of aged oak, they lasted about eight years before requiring major repair. Horses could pull more weight on a plank road because of reduced friction, but they often became tired and sore on long journeys. The busier routes had two lanes, laid on separate beds of planks.

In 1847, Francis Schraudenbach received a territorial land grant to build a hotel with a tavern and dining room here. The inn catered to wealthy Milwaukee families vacationing in the area, and in 1889 it was purchased by Frederick Pabst, of the Pabst Brewing Company. He bestowed the name "Red Circle," which was part of the old Pabst brewing trademark. The original oak bar is still in use today. The Red Circle Inn offers elegant dining and specializes in Provimi veal.

4.0 Nashotah Park, to your left, has rest rooms and picnic tables. The next stretch passes between Okauchee and Moose Lakes.

6.3 Right onto County Highway K where County Highway C ends in the village of Stone Bank.

6.5 Continue straight on County Highway K at the junction with West Shore, by the cemetery.

8.1 Cross WI 83 and go straight onto Beaver Lake Road, which passes through the golf course and provides some beautiful views of Beaver Lake to your right.

9.7 Left onto County Highway E.

10.2 Left onto County Highway E where County Highway EF turns right.

10.7 Continue on County Highway E where it makes a 90-degree right turn at the junction with Red Fox.

11.3 The silhouette of Holy Hill can be seen off in the distance as you come down this hill.

11.7 Cross County Highway VV.

13.9 Monches Community Park is on your left. Rest rooms are available. The shorter option to Holy Hill starts here.

14.0 Keep left as County Highway E becomes Center Oak Street in Monches.
Settled predominantly by Irish Catholics in the early 1840s, Monches was origi-nally called O'Connellsville, after the great Irish emancipator Daniel O'Connell. You will notice many road names with an Irish theme and many Irish flags flying along this route. John Hartley, the town's first postmaster, renamed the town Monches, after a Native American leader.

14.2 The Monches Mill House (262-966-7546), a cozy bed-and-breakfast inn, sits reflectively on the banks of the village millpond.
Innkeepers Elaine and Harvey Taylor purchased this historic gem at auction in 1975, and its eclectic decor features art acquired on their frequent travels to France and the Caribbean. The Taylors live in a solar home behind the Mill House and raise vegetables, fruits, and eggs used in luncheons offered on Wednesdays and Fridays.

14.4 Krauski Glass is a stained glass workshop where commissioned work is done and classes are offered. Visitors are welcome.

14.5 Backtrack through Monches on Center Oak, past the Monches Mill House.
Rudy and Ony's Tavern is now the only canteen in town; in the 1890s, Monches supported three saloons and more than a dozen shops.

14.8 Left onto Hartley Road.
The first home on your right (also the dog pound) has several llamas and a camel in the backyard.

15.3 Cross County Highway Q and jog slightly to the right onto Monches Road.

17.5 Left onto St. Augustine Road by St. Paul's Church.
This wonderful, winding Rustic Road conjures up images of leprechauns lurking in the ground fog that gathers in the hollows. There is one steep downhill with switch-backs. Ride in control!

19.1 Stay left at the junction, still on St. Augustine Road (no sign here).

20.3 Left onto Emerald Road.

21.0 Right onto Donegal Road.

21.9 Right into the back entrance of Holy Hill. There is no identifying sign—look carefully for the white metal gate and the "Service Entrance" sign.

22.4 Right at the junction and continue to the parking lot.

22.6 Parking lot.
There is a picnic area here that is a good place to park bikes. The cafeteria is open for snacks and Sunday brunch.

The cathedral sits atop the area's largest kame—a glacial feature you won't soon forget after pedaling up it! The word kame *comes from the Scottish* coomb, *meaning steep hill. Kames were created when water swirled in gigantic eddies through holes that resembled reverse funnels in the glacial ice sheet.*

The origin of this magnificent Catholic shrine centers around a story about a young Frenchman named François Soubrio. As a young man studying for the priesthood in France, Soubrio fell in love with a pretty young maiden. They decided to marry, and despite vehement opposition from his family and the church, Soubrio renounced his priestly vows. While Soubrio was away on a trip, his fiancée married another suitor. When he found he had been forsaken by his betrothed, he killed her in a fit of anger. He then fled to Quebec, where he became a recluse in a monastery in the old city.

He remained there for years, tortured by remorse. While studying old French manuscripts in the monastery library, Soubrio read of the voyages of Marquette and Joliet through the Great Lakes waterways. He was particularly interested in a reference by Marquette to a lofty, cone-shaped hill that the explorer had climbed, raising a cross and dedicating it to his patron saint, Mary. Soubrio set out to rediscover this "holy hill," to re-erect the now-decayed cross and to seek his atonement.

Along the way he was stricken with a partial paralysis of his legs and was forced to complete the final stage of his journey on his knees. When he finally crawled through the dense woods to the summit, he spent the night praying to St. Mary. At dawn he rose from his knees to find his paralysis gone. News of the miracle spread, and people began to come, seeking relief from their own ailments. Their crutches are displayed in a small glass case. One day Soubrio disappeared, and it's said that his ghost is still seen kneeling before a cross.

In 1855, the Reverend Francis Paulhuber bought the land and later built a log chapel. The original building has been replaced by the brick structures that now stand on the summit of Holy Hill. These include a Romanesque church with balconies overlooking the glacial countryside, a religious gift shop, a cafeteria, and lodging for pilgrims who visit the shrine. Holy Hill is staffed by the Discalced Carmelite Friars (262-628-1838).

22.6 Exit Holy Hill the same way you came in. Left at the T intersection by the parking lot, opposite the car traffic.

23.2 Left onto Donegal Road at the white entrance gate.

24.3 Right onto Emerald Road.

27.0 Left onto County Highway K at the cemetery.
For the shorter option, continue straight on Highway K through Monches to Monches Community Park.

28.1 Right onto County Highway Q and up the hill.

28.4 Left onto County Line Road (the sign to the right differs).

29.2 Left onto Hoff Road.

29.5 Continue on Hoff Road where it bends to the right.

30.7 Right onto WI 83 where Hoff Road ends.

30.8 Straight onto County Highway CW where WI 83 veers right.

32.4 Left onto Stone Bank Road.

34.5 Stone Bank Community Park offers rest rooms and a picnic area.

34.9 Left onto County Highway K.

35.2 Right onto County Highway C.

37.5 Nashotah County Park.

41.2 Right onto Main Street in Delafield.

41.7 Right onto Cushing Park Road to your starting point.

Bicycle Repair Service

Wheel and Sprocket, 2740 Heritage Road, Delafield; 262-646-6300

4

Northern Kettle Moraine State Forest

- **DISTANCE:** 33.4 miles
- **TERRAIN:** Rolling to hilly

The landscape in this area, with its matchless variety of glacial features, reads like a geology textbook. Much of this tour takes place in the hilly, ice-carved countryside of the Kettle Moraine State Forest's northern unit. As part of the Ice Age National Scenic Reserve, the Kettle Moraine is under the jurisdiction of the National Park Service.

During the Wisconsin stage of glaciation, about 18,000 to 20,000 years ago, two fingerlike lobes of moving ice, the Green Bay lobe and the Lake Michigan lobe, collided along a northeast-southwest line near here. At their junction, billions of tons of sand, gravel, and rock were deposited as the ice slowly melted away, resulting in a long sinuous ridge, known as a moraine. The word *moraine* derives from the Spanish word *morro,* meaning "snout."

Other prominent glacial features include drumlins, which are teardrop-shaped hills; eskers, which are narrow snakelike ridges; and kames, which are cone-shaped hills. Before or after your bike ride, consider stopping at the Henry S. Reuss Ice Age Visitor Center (920-533-8322) south of Plymouth on WI 67, where a video brings the era of mastodons and massive ice sheets to life.

Plymouth, the pleasant little town where the tour begins, was once the center of the world cheese market. In 1918, the Wisconsin

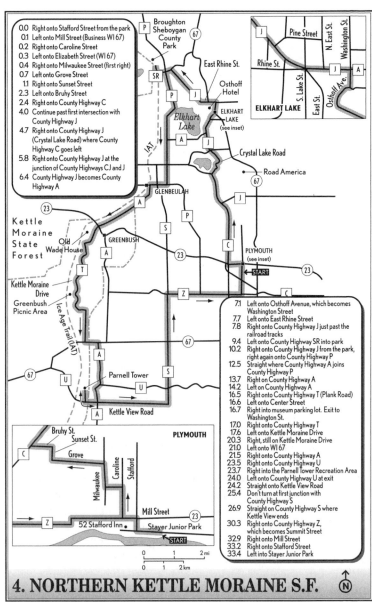

0.0 Right onto Stafford Street from the park
0.1 Left onto Mill Street (Business WI 67)
0.2 Right onto Caroline Street
0.3 Left onto Elizabeth Street (WI 67)
0.4 Right onto Milwaukee Street (first right)
0.7 Left onto Grove Street
1.1 Right onto Sunset Street
2.3 Left onto Bruhy Street
2.4 Right onto County Highway C
4.0 Continue past first intersection with County Highway J
4.7 Right onto County Highway J (Crystal Lake Road) where County Highway C goes left
5.8 Right onto County Highway J at the junction of County Highways CJ and J
6.4 County Highway J becomes County Highway A

Broughton Sheboygan County Park

East Rhine St.

Osthoff Hotel

Pine Street

N. East St.

Washington St.

J

Rhine St.

J

A

S. Lake St.

East St.

Osthoff Ave.

ELKHART LAKE

Elkhart Lake

ELKHART LAKE (see inset)

Crystal Lake Road

Road America

IAT

GLENBEULAH

Kettle Moraine State Forest

Old Wade House

GREENBUSH

Kettle Moraine Drive

Greenbush Picnic Area

Ice Age Trail (IAT)

Parnell Tower

Kettle View Road

PLYMOUTH (see inset)

START

7.1 Left onto Osthoff Avenue, which becomes Washington Street
7.7 Left onto East Rhine Street
7.8 Right onto County Highway J just past the railroad tracks
9.4 Left onto County Highway SR into park
10.2 Right onto County Highway J from the park, right again onto County Highway P
12.5 Straight where County Highway A joins County Highway P
13.7 Right on County Highway A
14.2 Left on County Highway A
16.5 Right onto County Highway T (Plank Road)
16.6 Left onto Center Street
16.7 Right into museum parking lot. Exit to Washington St.
17.0 Right onto County Highway T
17.6 Left onto Kettle Moraine Drive
20.3 Right, still on Kettle Moraine Drive
21.0 Left onto WI 67
21.5 Right onto County Highway A
23.5 Right onto County Highway U
23.7 Right into the Parnell Tower Recreation Area
24.0 Left onto County Highway U at exit
24.2 Straight onto Kettle View Road
25.4 Don't turn at first junction with County Highway S
26.9 Straight on County Highway S where Kettle View ends
30.3 Right onto County Highway Z, which becomes Summit Street
32.9 Right onto Mill Street
33.2 Right onto Stafford Street
33.4 Left into Stayer Junior Park

Bruhy St.

Sunset St.

Grove

PLYMOUTH

Milwaukee

Caroline

Stafford

Mill Street

52 Stafford Inn

Stayer Junior Park

START

0   1   2 mi
0   1   2 km

4. NORTHERN KETTLE MORAINE S.F.

Cheese Exchange, a kind of dairy board of trade, was established here to expand outlets for local cheesemakers. Plymouth remains at the hub of Wisconsin's cheese industry, with five large cheese factories, including the international headquarters of Sargento Cheese Company. Sargento was founded in 1848 when Leonard Gentine Sr. opened the Plymouth Cheese Counter in a small shed behind his funeral parlor, specializing in Italian cheeses.

To get to Plymouth, take WI 23 to Business WI 23, which becomes Mill Street as you enter town. Turn south onto Stafford Street and follow it to Stayer Junior Park, along the river, opposite 52 Stafford, An Irish Guest House. There is a grocery store behind the park.

0.0 Right onto Stafford Street from the park. On your left is 52 Stafford. *This is An Irish Guest House (920-893-0552), a charming bed-and-breakfast inn that offers luxury accommodations (whirlpool baths in every room), terrific food, and a lively Irish pub where bartenders are practiced in the art of pouring a pint of Guinness from the tap. Etched glass windows around the bar depict scenes of Celtic folklore, and guest rooms are named after Irish patriots, authors, politicians, and musicians.*

0.1 Left onto Mill Street (Business WI 67).

0.2 Right onto Caroline Street.

0.3 Left onto Elizabeth Street (still on WI 67).

0.4 Right onto Milwaukee Street (your first right).

0.7 Left onto Grove Street, passing the city park, which has rest rooms.

1.1 Right onto Sunset Street.

1.2 Continue straight at the stop sign, still on Sunset Street.

2.3 Left onto Bruhy Street.

2.4 Right onto County Highway C.
The headquarters of the Sargento Cheese Company are just after the turn.

4.0 Continue on County Highway C at the first intersection with County Highway J.

Glaciers formed the challenging hills on this route.

4.7 Right onto County Highway J (Crystal Lake Road) where County Highway C goes left (by the Crystal Lake sign).
This is a beautiful canopied road with lake views.

5.8 Right onto County Highway J at the junction of County Highways CJ and J.

6.4 County Highway J becomes County Highway A.

7.1 Left onto Osthoff Avenue toward Elkhart Lake. Don't take County Highways J and A, which veer to the right.
This pretty little resort town, originally called Elk Heart Lake, surrounds a beautiful lake of glacial origin. When the railroad reached here in 1860, Elkhart Lake became a popular summer vacation area for visitors from Milwaukee and Chicago. Auto races on the 4-mile track at Road America (1-800-365-RACE) draw competitors and racing aficionados from around the world. Portions of the movie Winning, with Paul Newman, were filmed here. Before the track was built, auto races were run through the streets of town!

7.5 Keep right by the Osthoff Hotel.

7.6 Osthoff Avenue becomes Washington Street.

7.7 Left onto East Rhine Street.

7.8 Right onto County Highway J just past the railroad tracks. Follow County Highway J out of town as it passes the gray grain elevator and the Kettle Moraine Scenic Drive sign.

9.4 Left onto County Highway SR into Broughton Sheboygan County Park.

9.7 The 13,000-acre Sheboygan Marsh is a favorite respite for Canada geese and other migrating waterfowl.
The Marsh Lodge restaurant serves breakfast. Rest rooms and picnic tables are available. Backtrack to the park exit.

10.2 Right onto County Highway J from the park. Then right immediately onto County Highway P.

11.4 Rest rooms are available here at the Elkhart Lake boat landing.

11.8 All Saint's Chapel.
This tiny stone Episcopal church in a picturesque oak grove holds services at 9 AM in June, July, and August.

12.5 Straight where County Highway A joins County Highway P.

13.7 Right on County Highway A through Glenbeulah.
This road parallels the glacier's terminal, or end moraine, which takes the form of a wooded ridge.

14.2 Left on County Highway A.

15.8 Terry's Bike Shop.

16.0 Cross WI 23 and continue on County Highway A to Greenbush.

16.5 Right onto County Highway T (Plank Road).

16.6 Left onto Center Street to the Wade House Stagecoach Inn and Wisconsin Carriage Museum (920-526-3271).

16.7 Right into the museum parking lot. Exit museum and go straight onto Washington Street.
The Wade House was built by Sylvanus Wade in 1851 to serve stagecoach traffic

on the busy Sheboygan to Fond du Lac Plank Road. The site is open daily May through October and offers ongoing demonstrations of spinning, blacksmithing, and candle-making by costumed interpreters. The Wisconsin Carriage Museum, one of the country's largest collections of restored horse-drawn carriages and wagons, is also on the property. Straight on Washington Street from the museum.

17.0 Right onto County Highway T.

17.6 Left onto Kettle Moraine Drive.
Gear down for a 1-mile climb. Continue past the group campsites and recreation areas to the picnic area at the summit.

19.4 Stop for a breather at the Greenbush picnic area, which has hiking trails, a picnic area, and rest rooms.

20.2 Don't descend so fast that you whiz by one of the Kettle Moraine's most striking glacial features, the Greenbush Kettle.
A sign marks the location to your right near the bottom of the hill. The kettle was formed when a giant, detached ice block buried under glacial debris melted. This steep-walled cavity is nearly as deep as it is wide.

20.3 Right, still on Kettle Moraine Drive, at the bottom of the hill.

21.0 Left onto WI 67. Take care, this is a busy road.

21.5 Right onto County Highway A.

23.5 Right onto County Highway U.

23.7 Right into the Parnell Tower Recreation Area, where you will find a picnic area, rest rooms, and a 50-foot wooden observation tower, from which you can survey the surrounding glacial topography.

24.0 Left onto County Highway U at exit.

24.2 Straight at the stop sign across County Highways A and U onto Kettle View Road.

25.4 Don't turn at first junction with County Highway S.

26.9 Straight on County Highway S where Kettle View ends.

27.5 The Silver Springs Restaurant (920-893-0969) offers fresh trout.

28.5 Cross WI 67. Take care, this is a busy road.

30.3 Right onto County Highway Z, which becomes Summit Street as you enter Plymouth.

32.9 Right onto Mill Street.
As you come down the hill into town, glance to the right at the giant fiberglass Holstein that celebrates Plymouth's dairy heritage. Considered the premier dairy cow, the Holstein was imported to Wisconsin from Holland in 1870.

33.2 Right onto Stafford Street.

33.4 Left into Stayer Junior Park.

Bicycle Repair Service

Back Door Bike Shop, 828 Eastern Avenue, Plymouth; 920-893-9786

Terry's Bike Shop, County Highway A, Greenbush; 920-526-3478

SOUTHWESTERN WISCONSIN

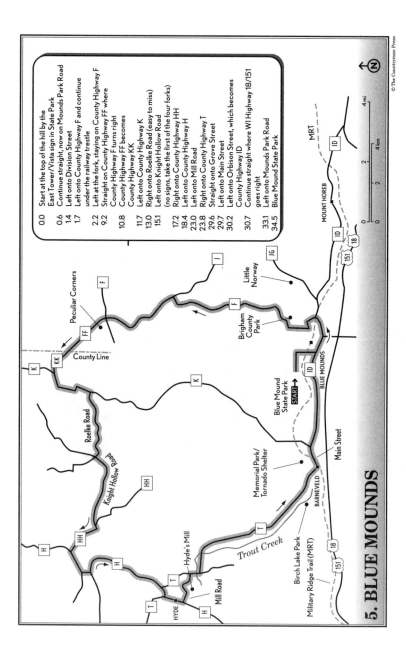

0.0	Start at the top of the hill by the East Tower/Vista sign in State Park
0.6	Continue straight, now on Mounds Park Road
1.4	Left onto Division Street
1.7	Left onto County Highway F and continue under the railway trestle
2.2	Left at the fork, staying on County Highway F
9.2	Straight on County Highway FF where County Highway F turns right
10.8	County Highway FF becomes County Highway KK
11.7	Left onto County Highway K
13.0	Right onto Roelke Road (easy to miss)
15.1	Left onto Knight Hollow Road (no signs, take the first of the four forks)
17.2	Right onto County Highway HH
18.4	Left onto County Highway H
23.0	Left onto Mill Road
23.8	Right onto County Highway T
29.6	Straight onto Grove Street
29.7	Left onto Main Street
30.2	Left onto Orbison Street, which becomes County Highway ID
30.7	Continue straight where WI Highway 18/151 goes right
33.1	Left onto Mounds Park Road
34.5	Blue Mound State Park

5. BLUE MOUNDS

Blue Mounds

- **DISTANCE:** 34.5 miles
- **TERRAIN:** Rolling to hilly

"I took view of some mountains . . . I ascended these and had an extensive view of the country," reported Jonathan Carver, an Englishman exploring the Wisconsin River Valley in 1776.

Mountains? Well, not quite. But the Blue Mounds, two bluish-gray hills that were important landmarks for pioneer travelers, still dominate the skyline of southwestern Wisconsin. Blue Mound State Park, located atop the westernmost of the two mounds, is the highest point in southern Wisconsin at 1,716 feet. The mounds are made of limestone, which has hardened over millions of years, forming a protective cap and slowing the weathering process.

The Blue Mounds area is known for its deep, sheltered valleys. Your face may be dampened by droplets of foggy mist as you descend into a hollow and quickly dried as you pedal out of the valley onto a plateau with open fields and warm sunshine. Perhaps it is this magical quality that attracted so many Norwegian settlers, with their penchant for elves and trolls, to the area.

Norse descendants in search of their roots may want to visit several attractions that are nearby but not on this route. Little Norway (608-437-8211), located on County Highway JG, encompasses a genuine Norwegian farmstead dating from 1856 and a traditional stavekirke (wooden church) that was part of Norway's exhibit at the 1893 Columbia Exposition in Chicago. Stop in at Schubert's Bakery in Mount Horeb for a loaf of limpa bread or a nourishing lunch of Norwegian meatballs. Mount Horeb also has a folk museum and about a dozen antiques emporiums.

Be prepared for a number of steep grades on this ride. The weak-kneed may need to walk a few uphill stretches but will still have the pleasure of whizzing down the other side. If you prefer more level terrain, the Military Ridge Trail traverses this area on the flat surface of an abandoned railroad bed.

Keep an eye on the sky if you take this trip on a hot, humid summer day—the area has a reputation for being a "tornado alley." You will pedal past the still-visible devastation of a 1984 twister later in the ride.

The tour begins at Blue Mound State Park, about 1 mile northwest of the village of Blue Mounds. Take WI 151 to Blue Mounds, exit north on County Highway F, and follow it to County Highway ID, where you turn left. This will take you to Mounds Park Road, where you should turn right and follow the signs into the park. Proceed to the picnic area at the top of the hill. Park facilities include an outdoor swimming pool with showers and changing rooms. Call the park office (608-437-5711) for camping reservations on holiday weekends.

0.0 The ride starts at the top of the hill by the East Tower/Vista sign in Blue Mound State Park.
Begin with a great downhill glide past the ranger station and into the town of Blue Mounds.

0.6 Continue straight at the stop sign at the park exit. You are now on Mounds Park Road.

1.4 Left onto Division Street.
The village of Blue Mounds was settled by Ebenezer Brigham in 1828. Brigham was the first white settler in the area and sought his fortune as a prospector. When other miners began to arrive, he turned to innkeeping, offering food and lodging along the old Military Ridge Trail. Brigham was also a colonel during the Blackhawk War and prominent in the development of Wisconsin statehood.

Today, Blue Mounds is a sleepy little burg with a church, pub, and convenience

Hyde's Mill is owned by a descendant of the original miller.

store. Stop in at the Hooterville Tavern after your ride for some good Wisconsin hospitality. No frosted mugs here—belly up to the bar, drink from the bottle, and find out who's pitching for the Brewers today.

1.7 Left onto County Highway F and continue under the railway trestle. There is no road sign, but there is a sign pointing toward Mazomanie and Brigham Park. Proceed in that direction.

2.2 Left at the fork, staying on County Highway F.

2.8 Stop to enjoy a panoramic view here at Brigham Park.
Land for the park was donated by Charles Brigham, a descendant of the village founder. On a clear day you can see 35 miles north toward the Wisconsin River Valley. Brigham Park also contains several mature sugar maples, rarely seen in southern Wisconsin.

2.8 Continue on County Highway F.
You're in for a treat now—there's a 4-mile downhill run ahead. Halfway down the hill, you'll pass the Saint James Catholic cemetery, with graves dating from the late 1800s.

7.0 Continue straight on County Highway F at the County Highway J junction.

9.2 Straight on County Highway FF where County Highway F turns right.
Anything seem strange? You have arrived at Peculiar Corners. In 1898, a post office named Peculiar was established in the farmhouse of Tom Davies. Not surprisingly, cyclists relish having their picture taken in front of the Peculiar Corners sign.

10.8 Continue straight when you enter Iowa County. County Highway FF now becomes County Highway KK.

11.7 Left onto County Highway K.

13.0 Right onto Roelke Road. The small sign here is easy to miss. If you come to the round barn, you have passed the turn.

15.1 Left onto Knight Hollow Road. There are no signs here, but Knight Hollow is the first of the four forks you see. Talk about a peculiar corner!

17.2 Right onto County Highway HH where Knight Hollow Road ends.

18.4 Left onto County Highway H where County Highway HH ends.
As you round the corner, you'll pass the historic Mill Creek Cheese Factory. Continue about 4.5 miles to the tiny village of Hyde.

23.0 Left onto Mill Road.
If you come to the Hyde Store, you've missed the turn to the mill. Stop for a snack or cool drink and backtrack to Mill Road. Hyde's Mill was built in 1850 by Theodore Sawle. The old millstones used to grind grain are lined up next to the road. If you are lucky, Ted Sawle, a descendant of the original miller, will come out and give you a tour of the mill and his fully equipped blacksmith shop. He also has a water-powered generator that provides electricity to the local utility.

23.3 Continue straight on Mill Road.

23.8 Right onto County Highway T. This takes you through a beautiful valley along the Trout Creek public fishing area.

28.9 To your right is Birch Lake Park, which has rest rooms and a picnic area. From the park, you have a steep climb up to the village of Barneveld.

29.6 Straight onto Grove Street at the hilltop.

29.7 Left onto Main Street.

30.1 Memorial Park.
The first thing that you'll notice about Barneveld is its bald appearance. There are very few large trees, and the town's modern ranch and split-level homes look oddly out of place amid older farm communities. Though the buildings are new, the village was founded many years ago. What you see is evidence of the powerful tornado that swept down on Barneveld on June 8, 1984, killing nine people and destroying three churches, the entire commercial district, and 60 percent of the homes.

Residents rallied to the motto "we're not giving up—we're going on." With the help of federal disaster funds they worked together to rebuild the entire town. The park and tornado shelter were built in memorial to those who died. The shelter contains pictures of the downtown area following the tornado, a covered picnic area, and rest rooms.

This route continues back via the roadway. However, you may opt to return to Blue Mounds on the Military Ridge Trail. This adds a mile to the trip.

30.2 Left onto Orbison Street. This turns into County Highway ID.

30.7 Continue straight where WI Highway 18/151 goes right.

33.1 Left onto Mounds Park Road toward Blue Mound State Park.

33.9 Continue straight and up, up, up into the park.

34.5 Once you've caught your breath, survey the area you've just covered from the park's two 40-foot observation towers.
Vistas extend as far as the Wisconsin–Iowa border on a clear day. These towers were originally built for another purpose. Vacationers traveled to the area by train from Chicago to watch horses race on a half-mile oval here—the road through the picnic area roughly traces the circuit. The towers offered box-seat viewing for race patrons.

Bicycle Repair Service

Dan Atkins Bicycle Shoppe, 517 Half Mile Road, Verona; 608-845-6644

6

Spring Green/Wisconsin River/ Frank Lloyd Wright Country

- **DISTANCE:** 22.5 (without visit to Global View) or 31.4 miles
- **TERRAIN:** Rolling to hilly

The Spring Green valley was home to architectural genius Frank Lloyd Wright, and the area's pleasing landscape served as his inspiration. Blending in with the rugged bluffs and tucked into niches of wooded hillside are the flat-roof profiles, cantilever projections, and steeplelike spires that identify the designs of Wright and his apprentices.

Unlike his buildings, Wright's lifestyle did not mesh harmoniously with the Spring Green hills. His cohabitation with his mistress, Mamah Borthwick Cheney, was considered scandalous by conservative local standards. After the death of Mamah Cheney in a tragic fire at Taliesin, Wright was married twice and was eventually accepted by the community. Older residents still remember the eccentric shadow Wright cast as he strolled about town in a swirling black cape and carrying a walking stick.

Lodging is available in several local motels, including two designed by students of Wright, the Usonian Inn (608-588-2323) and the Round Barn (608-588-2568). The Spring Green General Store & Café, on Albany Street in Spring Green, is a local gathering spot offering hearty, homemade food and unusual gift items.

The steep hills and narrow winding valleys of this unglaciated part of Wisconsin often prompt comparisons to Vermont. Those who undertake this ride should have a good understanding of

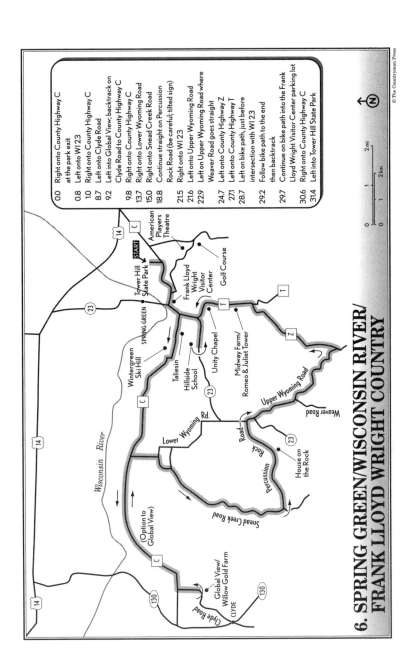

6. SPRING GREEN/WISCONSIN RIVER/ FRANK LLOYD WRIGHT COUNTRY

0.0	Right onto County Highway C at the park exit
0.8	Left onto WI 23
1.0	Right onto County Highway C
8.7	Left onto Clyde Road
9.2	Left into Global View; backtrack on Clyde Road to County Highway C
9.8	Right onto County Highway C
13.7	Right onto Lower Wyoming Road
15.0	Right onto Snead Creek Road
18.8	Continue straight on Percussion Rock Road (be careful; tilted sign)
21.5	Right onto WI 23
21.6	Left on Upper Wyoming Road
22.9	Left on Upper Wyoming Road where Weaver Road goes straight
24.7	Right onto County Highway Z
27.1	Left onto County Highway T
28.7	Left on bike path, just before intersection with WI 23
29.2	Follow bike path to the end and then backtrack
29.7	Continue on bike path into the Frank Lloyd Wright Visitor Center parking lot
30.6	Right onto County Highway C
31.4	Left into Tower Hill State Park

© The Countryman Press

their gears, a dependable pair of knees, and a fair degree of confidence on downhill stretches. A summertime ritual for many cyclists from nearby Madison, this ride offers a near-perfect combination of the corporal and cerebral—an afternoon of challenging cycling with stops to admire Wright's masterpieces, followed by a cleansing dip in the Wisconsin River, a sunset picnic on the river's shores, and an evening of Shakespeare under the stars at American Players Theatre.

The tour begins at Tower Hill State Park (608-588-2116). If you are heading west on WI 14, turn onto County Highway C and follow it south for about 1 mile to the park. The park is open from May through October and has campsites, hiking trails, a canoe landing, and pit toilets.

Tower Hill Park marks the site of the abandoned village of Helena. When lead was discovered in nearby hills in the 1830s, residents of Helena hung their hopes on a thriving new industry, the manufacture of lead shot. Molten lead was poured through strainers and dropped down a 120-foot shaft into a pool of cold water, where it formed into round pellets. The shot was sorted by size and shipped out for use in the Civil War. A short hike from the parking area takes you to the shot tower and a scenic overlook of the Wisconsin River.

0.0 Right onto County Highway C at the park exit.

0.1 To your left is the entrance to American Players Theatre and the House on the Rock Resort and Golf Course.
American Players Theatre (608-588-2361) performs the work of Shakespeare and other great playwrights in a spectacular natural setting. The bowl-shaped, multi-tiered theater is nestled in a wooded hillside where whippoorwills, bullfrogs, falling stars, and fireflies provide the special effects. There is a pleasant picnic area adjacent to the parking area where theatergoers can enjoy a pre-performance repast.

0.7 To your right is a wonderful view of the lower Wisconsin River. To your left is the Frank Lloyd Wright Visitor Center and Café (608-588-7900).
As you look downstream, imagine pinery boys navigating heavily laden lumber rafts around the ever-shifting sandbars. These days the sandbars are populated

with sunning canoeists, campers, and snapping turtles. Directly across the river is a beach where you can swim after the ride.

The visitor center is housed in a building designed by Wright and constructed posthumously from his plans. Here you can sign up for any of four different tours of the Taliesin buildings and grounds. There is also a gift shop, an exhibit area, and a café that serves breakfast and lunch from a creative menu featuring fresh local products. Restaurant furnishings are Wright-inspired, and most tables face the river.

0.8 Left onto WI 23. Use caution, this is a busy road.

1.0 Right onto County Highway C.

1.2 Taliesin is to your left.
Taliesin (tally-ehssen) means "shining brow" in Welsh, the language of Wright's relatives. He chose a high spot on his mother's property for his home, a stunning example of prairie-style architecture, often referred to as his "autobiography in wood and stone." Taliesin was twice destroyed by fire and rebuilt.

In response to mounting public concern over the deterioration of this architectural treasure, the Taliesin Preservation Commission was formed in 1990 to preserve the buildings and grounds. The state has committed more than 8 million dollars to the ongoing preservation project.

1.9 To the right is the entrance to Wintergreen Ski Area. A series of switchbacks on a paved road will lead you to the top for a panoramic view of the Wisconsin River Valley.

2.3 Enjoy this downhill stretch, still on County Highway C.

4.8 Junction with Lower Wyoming Road. If you do not wish to visit Global View (described below), turn left here and skip to the 13.7-mile mark. You will eliminate 8.9 miles of the ride. Otherwise, continue straight on County Highway C.

8.7 Left onto Clyde Road.

9.2 Left into Global View. Backtrack on Clyde Road to County Highway C.
Global View (608-583-5311) is a bazaar in a barn, an incongruous yet interesting enterprise in the midst of the Wisconsin countryside. The shop features hand-selected, handcrafted clothing, jewelry, and textiles from India, Nepal, Thailand, Indonesia, and other Asian countries. The shop is located on Willow Gold Farm, a

Author Jane Hall in the Spring Green Valley

pleasant place for lunch. Picnic tables and rest rooms are provided. Exit from the parking lot to the right on Clyde Road and backtrack to County Highway C.

9.8 Right onto County Highway C.

13.7 Right onto Lower Wyoming Road.

15.0 Right onto Snead Creek Road.

16.2 Splendid valley views and picturesque farms to your right for the next 2 miles.
Be sure to stop occasionally and look back at where you've been.

18.8 Continue straight on Percussion Rock Road where it meets Snead Creek Road. Don't turn off to the right here; tilted signs may cause confusion.

21.5 Right onto WI 23 for very short distance.
Before turning, glance back at Percussion Rock, the massive, granite outcropping that gives the road its name. You may also be able to spot the horizontal glass pinnacle of the House on the Rock's "Infinity Room," which projects out over the surrounding countryside. It's on the left side of the road as you look back and is easiest to see when leaves on the trees are sparse.

The House on the Rock (608-935-3639) was built in the 1940s by sculptor and collector Alex Jordan. It took more than 5,000 tons of stone to construct the original building, which consists of 13 rooms, each on a different level. Opened to the public in 1961, today's House on the Rock is a museum complex housing Jordan's personal collections of mechanical musical devices, dolls, guns, and Oriental art, as well as the world's largest carousel. It's not advisable to bike to the entrance, about 2 miles south on WI 23—the traffic is too heavy. If it sounds interesting, return later by car.

21.6 Left onto Upper Wyoming Road.

22.9 Left on Upper Wyoming Road where Weaver Road goes straight.
This road winds through a beautiful valley, followed by a wooded uphill stretch.

24.7 Left onto County Highway Z and enjoy a great downhill.

27.1 Left onto County Highway T.

28.3 To the left you will see Midway Farm in the foreground, with the Romeo and Juliet Tower behind it.
The 56-foot tower is actually a windmill that stood up to gusty southwest winds for 92 years before it was dismantled and restored in 1991. The windmill was Wright's first attempt at building a structure with no internal bracing, a concept with which he continued to experiment throughout his career. The interlocking diamond and octagon shapes provide the windmill with strength and account for its name, explained in Wright's autobiography. "Romeo will do all the work and Juliet will cuddle along to support and exalt him," he said of the windmill's construction.

28.6 To the left is Unity Chapel and a small cemetery.
This picturesque stone chapel was built in 1866 by the Lloyd-Jones family, including Anna Lloyd-Jones, Frank Lloyd Wright's mother. A contemporary metal sculpture identifies the burial spot of Frank Lloyd Wright. Wright was originally laid to rest here, but his body was later disinterred and moved to Phoenix, Arizona, for burial beside his last wife at Taliesin West. Gravestones for many of his Welsh relatives, most of them named Jones, as well as for Mamah Cheney, are found here.

28.7 Left onto bike path, just before the intersection with WI 23.

29.2 Follow bike path to the end. Across the road you will see Hillside Home School.
The school was built by Wright for his aunts, Jane and Nell Lloyd-Jones, who oper-

ated a progressive coed boarding school here. Built of native oak and sandstone, it is a classic example of Wright's fondness for natural building materials. The building is now the summer home of the Frank Lloyd Wright Foundation, which operates a professional architectural firm as well as a school of architecture.

Turn around and backtrack on the bike path.

29.7 Cross County Highway T. Continue on the bike path as it leads you into the Frank Lloyd Wright Visitor Center parking lot.

30.6 Right onto County Highway C from the visitor center.

31.4 Left into Tower Hill State Park.

Bicycle Repair Service

None in this area.

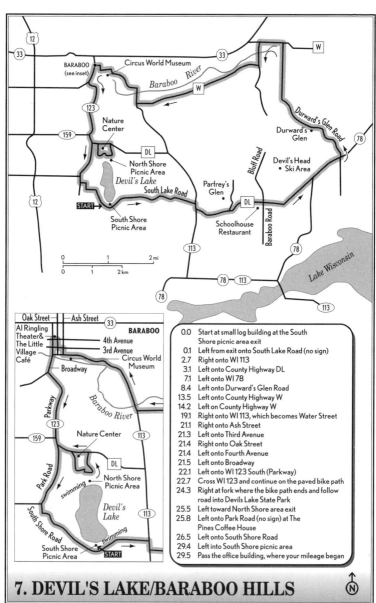

0.0	Start at small log building at the South Shore picnic area exit
0.1	Left from exit onto South Lake Road (no sign)
2.7	Right onto WI 113
3.1	Left onto County Highway DL
7.1	Left onto WI 78
8.4	Left onto Durward's Glen Road
13.5	Left onto County Highway W
14.2	Left on County Highway W
19.1	Right onto WI 113, which becomes Water Street
21.1	Right onto Ash Street
21.3	Left onto Third Avenue
21.4	Right onto Oak Street
21.4	Left onto Fourth Avenue
21.5	Left onto Broadway
22.1	Left onto WI 123 South (Parkway)
22.7	Cross WI 123 and continue on the paved bike path
24.3	Right at fork where the bike path ends and follow road into Devils Lake State Park
25.5	Left toward North Shore area exit
25.8	Left onto Park Road (no sign) at The Pines Coffee House
26.5	Left onto South Shore Road
29.4	Left into South Shore picnic area
29.5	Pass the office building, where your mileage began

7. DEVIL'S LAKE/BARABOO HILLS

© The Countryman Press

Devil's Lake/Baraboo Hills

- **DISTANCE:** 29.5 miles
- **TERRAIN:** Rolling to hilly

"Here, in a tremendous gorge . . . hemmed in on all sides by frowning rocks, of prodigious size, piled up in every conceivable form, nestles one of the loveliest sheets of water in the whole world." This is how Rand McNally's *Tourist Guide to the Northwest*, published in the 1880s, described Devil's Lake. Other tourist literature of that era compared Devil's Lake to California's Lake Tahoe in appearance and origin.

Devil's Lake State Park and the adjacent Baraboo Hills offer some of the most dramatic scenery and challenging cycling in Wisconsin. The lake is situated in a mile-long gap, surrounded on three sides by 500-foot quartzite bluffs. Geologists tell us that the opening was carved by an ancient channel of the Wisconsin River. When the Wisconsin Glacier descended, it rerouted the river outside of the bluffs and deposited a dam of rocks and dirt at each of the two open ends, creating an enclosed basin. The result was a 50-foot-deep, crystal-clear, spring-fed lake, known today as Devil's Lake.

Winnebago Indian legends provide more action-packed versions of the lake's creation. One tale describes a meteor striking with such force that it sinks deep into the earth, displacing an enormous amount of rock and debris. The meteor's impact is followed by a great rain, which fills the cavernous pit with water. Another legend tells of thunderbirds flying high above the lake, launching lightning bolts into the water and onto the bluffs. Angry water spirits retaliate by hurling rocks and waterspouts into the air. This battle accounts for the cracked and tumbled rock faces on the bluffs.

Winnebago Indians called the lake *Ta-wa-cun-chuk-dah,* which translates as Sacred Lake or Spirit Lake. The present name, Devil's Lake, is thought to be a name invented by turn-of-the-century ad men, who hoped to lure tourists to this nascent resort area with a promise of adventure. Unfortunately, it implies that early Native Americans feared or shunned the lake. In fact, effigy mounds in animal shapes along the South Shore are evidence that it was revered.

Devil's Lake and its surroundings were designated as a state park in 1911. Now attracting more than a million visitors a year, it is the busiest park in the Midwest. If you plan to camp, be sure to call the park office (608-356-8301) for campsite reservations. Visiting midweek or slightly off-season will also help avoid the crowds. In addition to cycling on park roads, the park offers several mountain-biking loops on cross-country ski trails. Most cyclists follow a bike ride with a refreshing swim. The bluffs beckon casual day hikers as well as skilled rock climbers. Step carefully, though, to avoid a sunning timber rattlesnake!

This tour begins at the park's South Shore picnic area. Take WI 113 to South Lake Road, turn left if coming from the south or right if coming from the north, and continue to the South Shore entrance.

0.0 Mileage begins at the small log office building at the exit for the South Shore picnic area.
There are rest rooms, changing facilities, a concession stand, and picnic shelter here.

There were once three large hotels on the South Shore, with a total of several hundred rooms. A daily train dropped tourists at their doorsteps until the automobile became popular. Old travel posters advertised Devil's Lake as "just the place where tired brain workers may rest and get strong," a slogan that's still amazingly apt today.

0.1 Left from exit onto South Lake Road (no sign here).
To your left the bluff is covered with loose rock, called talus. This has broken away because of pressure created by tree roots and ice. Enjoy a pleasant coast downhill and out of the park.

2.7 Right onto WI 113.

3.1 Left onto County Highway DL.

5.1 If you wish to visit Parfrey's Glen Scientific Area, turn left here.
A short hike ($\frac{1}{2}$ mile, round-trip) through this sheltered glen is very worthwhile, especially on a hot summer day. "Glen" is a Scottish word for a narrow, rocky ravine. "Parfrey" comes from Robert Parfrey, an Englishman who acquired the property in 1865. The glen's walls are sandstone, embedded with pebbles and boulders of quartzite. This quartzite conglomerate is often called "plum pudding" stone because quartzite "plums" are cemented in sandstone "pudding." This composition is proof that the glen was once submerged in an ancient sea.

Because cool air is trapped in the glen, the plants found here are more typical of the northern part of Wisconsin. Examples are yellow birch, mountain maple, and red elder. The bamboolike plant that forms low thickets along the creek is scouring rush, a relative of ferns. The presence of silica in the stem enabled pioneers to scour pots and pans with it. Lichens, rarely found in cities because of their sensitivity to air pollutants, grow abundantly here.

5.4 At the intersection with Bluff Road, the Schoolhouse Restaurant is immediately to your right, and Devil's Head Resort is about 1 mile to your left. Turn only if you're hungry or interested in exploring.
The Schoolhouse Restaurant is a conglomerate of another sort—a historic schoolhouse, a jail house, a Lutheran church, and a railroad caboose—that have been patched together to make this popular eatery. The outdoor deck is a pleasant place to enjoy a pizza on a warm day. Devil's Head Lodge is a full-service resort that offers skiing in the winter and golf in the summer.

7.1 Left onto WI 78 where County Highway DL ends.

8.4 Left onto Durward's Glen Road.

9.4 Left, following the sign to Durward's Glen.

9.6 Visitor parking area at Durward's Glen.
The lovely chapel built of hand-hewn logs and the surrounding gardens and trickling

Winnebago Indians called Devil's Lake Ta-wa-cun-chuk-dah, *which means Sacred Lake or Spirit Lake.*

brook were willed to the Roman Catholic order of St. Camillus about 70 years ago. The order's primary mission is the healing of the sick, and facilities here are now used for nondenominational workshops and retreats focusing on personal and spiritual growth. The order asks that visitors to Durward's Glen cooperate in maintaining an atmosphere of silence and meditation.

Exit Durward's Glen to the left, and return 0.2 mile to Durward's Glen Road.

9.8 Left onto Durward's Glen Road. At the crest of the hill, you are crossing the spine of the Baraboo Range. A 2-mile downhill run follows.

13.5 Left onto County Highway W.

14.2 Left on County Highway W, following the Baraboo River. County Highway X goes straight here.

19.1 Right onto WI 113, which becomes Water Street when you enter Baraboo.

20.8 To your left is the Circus World Museum. Opposite the museum is Ringlingville Park, which has picnic tables.

Here along the banks of the Baraboo River are the old brick and wooden buildings where circus workers trained animals, practiced stunts, and carried out off-season repairs from 1884 to 1918, when this sleepy little town served as the winter home of Ringling Brothers and Barnum and Bailey's "Greatest Show on Earth." Baraboo was the birthplace of the five Ringling brothers, whose modest carnival act grew into an enormous enterprise, eventually allowing them to buy out their competition, the Barnum and Bailey troupe.

Today, the Circus World Museum (608-356-0800), owned by the Wisconsin State Historical Society, occupies this spot and offers a fascinating look back at the days when everyone's summer centered around the circus coming to town. Highlights include the museum's 50 meticulously restored circus parade wagons and the daily big-top show, complete with charismatic ringmaster, death-defying trapeze artists, exotic wild animals, and ebullient clowns. Other exhibits and demonstrations depict interesting aspects of circus life. The museum is open daily, May through October.

21.1 Right onto Ash Street to start the loop around Baraboo's historic city square.

21.3 Left onto Third Avenue.

21.4 Right onto Oak Street.

21.4 Left onto Fourth Avenue.
You pass the Al Ringling Theater on your right, built by one of the famous circus siblings for $100,000 in 1915. Modeled after a European opera house, it now functions as a movie theater.

The Little Village Café, on the corner of Fourth Street and Broadway, is a great place to stop for lunch. The restaurant has outdoor tables overlooking the town square and a menu that includes Mexican items, pastas, and sandwiches. The building that houses the café is a historic site in the history of journalism. Ansel N. Kellogg, editor of the Baraboo News Republic (which has the present-day distinction of being the state's smallest daily), was dismayed when his partner quit to join Union forces in the Civil War. He kept the newspaper afloat by ordering two pages of preprinted war news each week and printing local news on the reverse side. The operation later developed into the nation's first news syndicate.

21.5 Left onto Broadway.

22.1 Left onto WI 123 South (Parkway).

22.7 Cross WI 123 carefully and resume cycling on the paved bike path.

24.3 Right at fork where the bike path ends. This takes you to Devil's Lake State Park.

24.9 The park Nature Center is to your left.
The center includes dioramas, relief maps, paintings, and other exhibits that depict the area's history and geologic formation.

25.3 The North Shore picnic area has a swimming beach and rest rooms.

25.5 Left toward North Shore area exit.

25.8 Left onto Park Road (no road sign) at The Pines Coffee House.

26.3 Cross County Highway DL, following signs to South Shore entrance.

26.5 Left onto South Shore Road.
Long uphill, followed by downhill with steep switchbacks. Ride in control!

29.4 Left into South Shore picnic area.

29.5 Pass the office building, where your mileage began.

Bicycle Repair Service

Middleton Cycle Shop, 6641 University Avenue, Middleton; 608-831-RIDE (7433)

8

Wisconsin Dells/ Aldo Leopold Country

- **DISTANCE:** 24.2 miles
- **TERRAIN:** Rolling

Wisconsin Dells is known for some of Wisconsin's most exquisite natural beauty and some of humankind's most obtrusive, albeit entertaining, additions to it. This tour steers clear of the waterslides and wax museums in favor of the "real" Dells, a spectacular 7-mile stretch of the Wisconsin River lined with cliffs, chasms, pillars, and towers of 500-million-year-old Cambrian sandstone.

The words *Dell, Dells,* and *Delton,* which appear in local place names, all derive from the French word *dalle,* meaning throat. Winnebego Indian legend provides a colorful explanation of the Dells' creation, claiming that a giant snake slithered along the path of the Wisconsin River, parting the rocks with its enormous weight and creating a deep, serpentine depression. Rock structures with imaginative names like Chapel Gorge, Devil's Elbow, Witches' Gulch, and Fat Man's Misery are best seen on boat excursions through the Upper and Lower Dells. Call Dells Boat Tours (608-254-8555), Soma's Dells Cruises (608-254-2628), or Mark Twain Upper Dells Tours (608-254-6080) for schedules and itineraries.

The trip includes a stop at the International Crane Foundation (608-356-9462), a world center for the study and preservation of these mystical birds. Try to time your visit with one of the guided

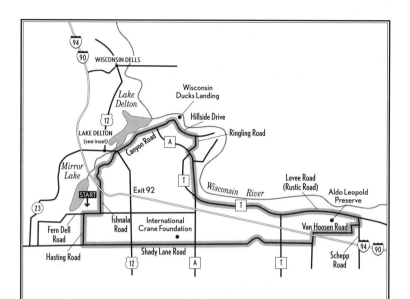

0.0	Exit the park at the ranger station and proceed straight onto Hasting Road
1.0	Left onto Shady Lane Road
3.7	Left into the International Crane Foundation (ICF)
8.3	Left onto Van Hoosen Road
10.1	Left onto Schepp Road
10.3	Left onto Levee Road
12.9	Right onto County Highway T
15.7	Right onto County Highway A
17.3	Right onto Ringling Road
17.9	Left onto Hillside Drive
19.6	Straight onto Canyon Road
21.2	Right onto East Adams Street
21.5	Left on Judson Street
21.6	Right onto WI 12 (Wisconsin Dells Parkway)
21.8	Left at the stoplight on Whitlock Street
21.9	Right onto West Delavan Street
22.1	Left onto South Burritt Avenue, which becomes Ishnala Road
23.9	Right onto Fern Dell Road
24.2	Right into Mirror Lake State Park

8. WISCONSIN DELLS/ ALDO LEOPOLD COUNTRY

© The Countryman Press

tours, which are given daily at 10 AM, 1 PM, and 3 PM from Memorial Day to Labor Day; and on weekends in May, September, and October. A self-guided tour is also possible.

Much of this route follows a rolling course along the Wisconsin River, passing the humble shack where Aldo Leopold was inspired to write his conservation classic, *A Sand County Almanac*. There are several picnic spots along the way and restaurants in the town of Lake Delton.

To reach Mirror Lake State Park, take I-90/94 to Exit 92 (WI 12). Follow WI 12 East for about ½ mile, then turn right on Fern Dell Road and continue for about 2½ miles to Mirror Lake State Park. The lake for which the park is named was once a millpond, formed by the damming of Dell Creek. Swimming is possible, although the water has a tannic cast. Reservations are suggested if you plan to camp at the park on a weekend (608-254-2333).

0.0 Exit the park at the ranger station and proceed straight onto Hasting Road.

1.0 Left onto Shady Lane Road.

2.5 Continue straight at the stop sign. Use caution crossing WI 12.

3.7 International Crane Foundation (ICF).
What looks like a housing development off in the distance is known as Crane City. These crane "condos" are home to some of the world's last remaining birds of several dwindling crane species, including the whooping crane and Siberian crane. ICF's leading-edge scientific research includes habitat preservation, captive breeding, and educational exchange programs on five continents. Allow about 1½ hours for a tour led by a well-informed aviculturist. The tour includes viewing of about 10 crane species in a display pod (they trumpet dramatic warning signals as you approach) and observing young cranes being walked by their "chick mamas"— humans partly or fully costumed as cranes who coach fledglings in the fundamentals of feeding and flying. Also on the premises are a restored prairie, picnic area, rest rooms, and gift shop.

Go left out of the parking lot, continuing on Shady Lane.

5.5 On your left is an abandoned church, now being used as a barn.

8.3 Left onto Van Hoosen Road.

8.4 Cross I-94.

8.5 You are now entering the Aldo Leopold Memorial Reserve.

10.1 Left onto Schepp Road.

10.3 Left onto Levee Road, designated a Rustic Road in 1987 in recognition of the 100th anniversary of ecologist Aldo Leopold's birth. You are now following the course of the Wisconsin River.

11.3 Look carefully off to your right and you will see Aldo Leopold's shack, hidden in the trees along the banks of the river.
The property belongs to Leopold's descendants and is not open to the public. Leopold lived in Wisconsin from 1924 to 1948 while working for the University of Wisconsin, first as associate director of the Forest Products Lab and later as chairman of the Game Management Department. He died of a heart attack at the age of 61, while fighting a prairie fire on a neighbor's land.

Leopold is best known as the author of A Sand County Almanac *and* Round River, *treatises on environmental ethics that have proven to be well ahead of their time. Having just toured the Crane Foundation, you will appreciate this passage from* A Sand County Almanac, *called "Marshland Elegy."*

A dawn wind stirs on the great marsh. With almost imperceptible slowness it rolls a bank of fog across the wide morass. Like the white ghost of a glacier the mists advance, riding over phalanxes of tamaracks, sliding across bog-meadows heavy with dew. A single silence hangs from horizon to horizon. Out of some far recess of the sky a tinkling of little bells falls soft upon the listening land. Then again silence. Now comes a baying of some sweet-throated sound, soon the clamor of a responding pack. Then a far clear blast of hunting horns, out of the sky into the fog.

High horns, low horns, silence, and finally a pandemonium of trumpets, rattles, croaks, and cries that almost shakes the bog with its nearness, but without yet disclosing whence it comes. At last a glint of sun reveals the approach of a great echelon of birds. On motionless wing they emerge from the lifting mists, sweep a final arc of sky, and settle in clangorous descending spirals to their feeding grounds. A new day has begun on the crane marsh.

12.9 Right onto County Highway T.

15.7 Right onto County Highway A.
This is a busy road.

17.3 Right onto Ringling Road.

17.9 Left onto Hillside Drive.

18.9 This driveway down to the river is an entry point for the Wisconsin Ducks, WWII amphibious landing craft vehicles that offer sight-seeing tours. *During the summer, you need only wait 5 or 10 minutes for one to appear.*

19.6 Straight onto Canyon Road.

21.2 Right onto East Adams Street into the village of Lake Delton. *Be careful—traffic is heavy here in the summer months. There are several restaurants where you can get a sandwich or a cool drink.*

21.5 Left on Judson Street.

21.6 Right onto WI 12 (Wisconsin Dells Parkway).

21.8 Left at the stoplight on Whitlock Street.

21.9 Right onto West Delavan Street.

22.0 To your left is the Lake Delton Fire Department Park. *Water, rest rooms, and picnic tables are available here.*

22.1 Left onto South Burritt Avenue (this becomes Ishnala Road).

23.9 Right onto Fern Dell Road.

24.2 Right into Mirror Lake State Park.

Bicycle Repair Service

Middleton Cycle Shop, 6641 University Avenue, Middleton; 608-831-RIDE (7433)

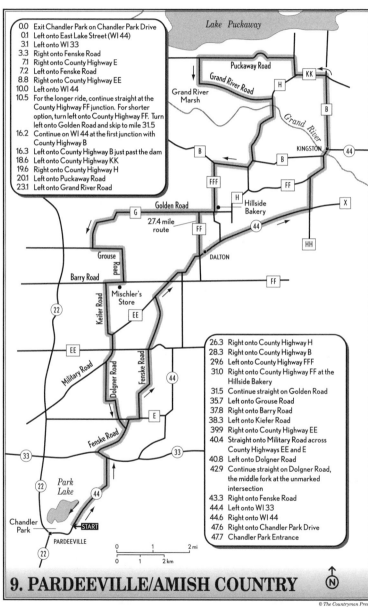

0.0	Exit Chandler Park on Chandler Park Drive
0.1	Left onto East Lake Street (WI 44)
3.1	Left onto WI 33
3.3	Right onto Fenske Road
7.1	Right onto County Highway E
7.2	Left onto Fenske Road
8.8	Right onto County Highway EE
10.0	Left onto WI 44
10.5	For the longer ride, continue straight at the County Highway FF junction. For shorter option, turn left onto County Highway FF. Turn left onto Golden Road and skip to mile 31.5
16.2	Continue on WI 44 at the first junction with County Highway B
16.3	Left onto County Highway B just past the dam
18.6	Left onto County Highway KK
19.6	Right onto County Highway H
20.1	Left onto Puckaway Road
23.1	Left onto Grand River Road

Lake Puckaway

Puckaway Road

Grand River Road

Grand River Marsh

KK

H

B

Grand River

KINGSTON

44

B

B

FFF

FF

H   Hillside Bakery

X

Golden Road

G

27.4 mile route

FF

44

HH

DALTON

Grouse Road

Barry Road

FF

Kiefer Road

Mischler's Store

EE

EE

Military Road

Dolgner Road

Fenske Road

44

E

33

Fenske Road

33

22

22

Park Lake

44

Chandler Park

START

PARDEEVILLE

22

26.3	Right onto County Highway H
28.3	Right onto County Highway B
29.6	Left onto County Highway FFF
31.0	Right onto County Highway FF at the Hillside Bakery
31.5	Continue straight on Golden Road
35.7	Left onto Grouse Road
37.8	Right onto Barry Road
38.3	Left onto Kiefer Road
39.9	Right onto County Highway EE
40.4	Straight onto Military Road across County Highways EE and E
40.8	Left onto Dolgner Road
42.9	Continue straight on Dolgner Road, the middle fork at the unmarked intersection
43.3	Right onto Fenske Road
44.4	Left onto WI 33
44.6	Right onto WI 44
47.6	Right onto Chandler Park Drive
47.7	Chandler Park Entrance

0   1   2 mi
0   1   2 km

9. PARDEEVILLE/AMISH COUNTRY

N

Pardeeville/Amish Country

- **DISTANCE:** 27.4 or 47.7 miles
- **TERRAIN:** Rolling

Bicycling brings you face-to-face with Wisconsin's Amish community on this tour through rolling farmland, where you'll encounter little traffic other than horse-drawn buggies. There are more than 500 Amish people in the area surrounding Kingston and Dalton. Most arrived in Wisconsin from the Shipshewana, Indiana, area in the mid-1970s; others came from Amish colonies in Pennsylvania. In contrast to other Amish settlements, the people who live here do not ride bicycles because of the rubber tires, which they consider an unnecessary luxury.

Most of the Amish are employed in farming or carpentry. Zucchini and other vegetables are raised for their own needs and sold to canning factories. Beautiful bentwood rockers and cedar chests are available from small shops in their homes. Groups of men also hire out to build non-Amish homes. Meticulously tended flower gardens stand in brilliant contrast to the stark colors of Amish dress and plain white paint of their buildings. The Amish are very private people and prefer not to be photographed; please don't do so without asking permission. All Amish-run shops are closed on Sunday. You'll also pass several Amish bakeries that are open only on Fridays and Saturdays.

There are very few commercial attractions along this route and, therefore, few notes for the ride. Just relax and take in the peaceful simplicity of the Amish countryside.

The tour begins at Chandler Park in Pardeeville. The park offers a swimming beach, picnic facilities, rest rooms, and water. To reach Pardeeville, take WI 51 north from Madison to WI 22. Follow WI 22 into Pardeeville and to the junction with WI 44. Turn right onto WI 44 (East Lake Street). The entrance to Chandler Park is on the left.

0.0 Exit Chandler Park on Chandler Park Drive. Mileage begins at the stone gate.

0.1 Left onto East Lake Street (WI 44) and follow it out of town.
You'll be riding around Park Lake.

1.1 Pass the Park Lake County Park boat landing.

3.1 Left onto WI 33 for a short distance.

3.3 Right onto Fenske Road.

7.1 Right onto County Highway E for 0.2 mile at the North Scott Baptist Church.

7.2 Left onto Fenske Road.
Many of the large white houses here are Amish homes, added onto many times to accommodate growing families. You may see draft horses in the fields—horses are used to pull buggies, harvest hay, and skid lumber.

8.8 Right onto County Highway EE.

10.0 Left onto WI 44. This is a busy road, but it has a good shoulder.

10.5 For the 47.7-mile ride, continue straight at the County Highway FF junction.
The village of Dalton is off to your left. Snacks are available at Pat's Corner Grocery.

For the 27.4-mile ride, turn left onto County Highway FF. Continue on County Highway FF through Dalton and for 1 mile north of town. Then turn left onto Golden Road and skip to the 31.5-mile mark for the remaining directions.

15.7 Enter the village of Kingston.
The Kingston House and Camelot Supper Club serve meals. There is no membership required for this supper "club," despite what the name implies.

A Sunday morning in Wisconsin's Amish country

16.2 Continue on WI 44 at the first junction with County Highway B.

16.3 Left onto County Highway B just past the dam.
Watch for the giant elk at a game farm a short distance down this road.

18.6 Left onto County Highway KK.

19.6 Right onto County Highway H where County Highway KK ends.

20.1 Left onto Puckaway Road.
Lake Puckaway is to your right and Grand River Marsh to your left. During the Ice Age, melting ice formed a depression that eventually filled with silt and decaying vegetation and ultimately became a marsh. When Wisconsin was first settled, the marsh was used for pasture and raising hay. When the land was acquired by the state, a dam was shut down, releasing enough water to flood 3,500 acres. The marsh is on a major flyway for ducks, geese, and sandhill cranes.

23.1 Left onto Grand River Road (a rougher paved road).

26.3 Right onto County Highway H where Grand River Road ends.

28.3 Right onto County Highway B.

29.6 Left onto County Highway FFF.

31.0 Right onto County Highway FF at the Hillside Bakery.

31.5 Continue straight on Golden Road where County Highway FF turns left. *This is where the 27.4-mile ride rejoins the 47.7-mile ride.*

35.7 Left onto Grouse Road.

37.8 Right onto Barry Road where Grouse Road ends. *Mischler's Country Store, which sells bulk foods for the Amish community, is just past the turn. Flours, sugars, spices, and fruit pie fillings are among the foodstuffs sold here. The store is closed on Sundays and Thursdays. Fresh baked goods are often sold here on Saturdays. There is also an Amish furniture shop across the road from Mischler's and a farmer's market a little farther down the road.*

38.3 Left onto Kiefer Road.

39.9 Right onto County Highway EE. Careful of the rumble strips and stop sign at the bottom of the hill.

40.4 Straight onto Military Road across County Highways EE and E.

40.8 Left onto Dolgner Road.

42.9 Continue straight on Dolgner Road, the middle fork at the unmarked intersection.

43.3 Right onto Fenske Road.

44.4 Left onto WI 33.

44.6 Right onto WI 44.

47.6 Right onto Chandler Park Drive.

47.7 Chandler Park entrance.

Bicycle Repair Service

None in this area.

CENTRAL
WISCONSIN

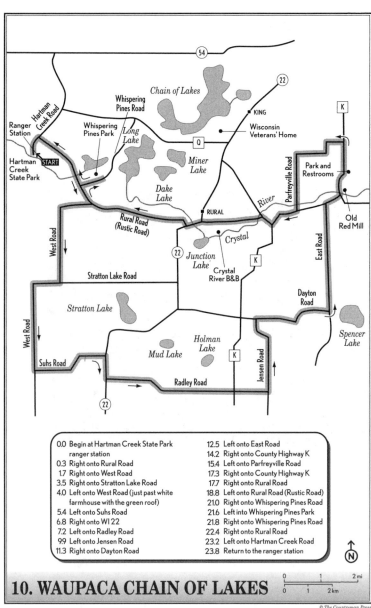

0.0	Begin at Hartman Creek State Park ranger station	12.5	Left onto East Road
0.3	Right onto Rural Road	14.2	Right onto County Highway K
1.7	Right onto West Road	15.4	Left onto Parfreyville Road
3.5	Right onto Stratton Lake Road	17.3	Right onto County Highway K
4.0	Left onto West Road (just past white farmhouse with the green roof)	17.7	Right onto Rural Road
		18.8	Left onto Rural Road (Rustic Road)
5.4	Left onto Suhs Road	21.0	Right onto Whispering Pines Road
6.8	Right onto WI 22	21.6	Left into Whispering Pines Park
7.2	Left onto Radley Road	21.8	Right onto Whispering Pines Road
9.9	Left onto Jensen Road	22.4	Right onto Rural Road
11.3	Right onto Dayton Road	23.2	Left onto Hartman Creek Road
		23.8	Return to the ranger station

10. WAUPACA CHAIN OF LAKES

Waupaca Chain of Lakes

- **DISTANCE:** 23.8 miles
- **TERRAIN:** Gently rolling

This tour takes you through a slice of central Wisconsin forest and farmland that lends itself well to old-fashioned, family-style fun. A lively summer resort area, most activity centers around a chain of 22 clear, spring-fed lakes, as well as numerous rivers and trout streams. Waupaca, the largest town near the Chain O' Lakes, probably took its name from the Native American words *Waubuck Seba,* meaning "pale or clear water." Keep an eye out for whitetails on this ride—the area has the state's highest deer population, and it's not unusual to startle a doe and fawn as you round a bend.

The trip begins at Hartman Creek State Park (715-258-2372), 1,200 acres of wooded countryside that skirt the terminal moraine of the Wisconsin Glacier. Wisconsin's cross-state Ice Age Trail passes through the park. Four spring-fed lakes were formed by the damming of Hartman Creek when the land was a private fish hatchery prior to becoming a state park. There is a swimming beach on Hartman Lake, and the park offers excellent facilities for family and group camping.

To reach Hartman Creek State Park, take WI 10 to Waupaca. From Waupaca, go west on WI 54 for about 4 miles, then left on Hartman Creek Road to the park.

0.0 The tour begins at the ranger station, near the park exit.

0.3 Right onto Rural Road.

1.7 Right onto West Road.

3.5 Right onto Stratton Lake Road.

4.0 Left onto West Road (no sign, but just past white farmhouse with the green roof).

5.4 Left onto Suhs Road.

6.8 Right onto WI 22. There is moderate traffic, but the road has a wide shoulder.

7.2 Left onto Radley Road.

9.9 Left onto Jensen Road.

11.3 Right onto Dayton Road.

12.5 Left onto East Road.

14.2 Right onto County Highway K where East Road ends.

14.8 The Old Red Mill Gift Shop, on the banks of the Crystal River, has an interesting history.
Built by James Lathrop in 1854, the mill ground feed and graham and buckwheat flour until 1960, when it was converted to the Red Mill Colonial Shop. The buyers of the mill, which now houses a shop selling early American furniture and gifts, were committed to restoring and maintaining the mill's massive 24-foot water wheel. After a long search, a 130-year-old white oak tree on an island near Fremont, Wisconsin, was selected to form a new hub for the wheel. The solid oak hub weighs a ton and a half; the spokes vary in weight from 90 to 120 pounds, depending on the density of the wood. Sixty buckets, set into the rim of the wheel, transport the water, creating a beautiful effect. Also on the Red Mill property is a replica of a covered bridge and a small chapel in the woods. Just beyond the mill, also on the river, is a pleasant park with rest rooms.

15.4 Left onto Parfreyville Road.

17.3 Right onto County Highway K.

17.7 Right onto Rural Road where County Highway K goes left.
Every Sunday afternoon you will find a row of lawn chairs set up along the river-

bank belonging to spectators who gather to watch paddlers navigate the small rapids here in tippy fiberglass canoes. If you have a yen to share the adventure, canoes can be rented from Ding's Dock (715-258-2612) on County Highway Q. The dock provides transportation to the river and pick-up at the end of the voyage.

18.8 Left onto Rural Road (Rustic Road) and follow it into the village of Rural. *The town was named by James Hinchman Jones, the first settler. He lived in a wooded area near the river and referred to his property as the "rural holdings." Rural was the halfway point on the stagecoach line between Berlin and Stevens Point. It grew up around a gristmill operated by Jones and a stagecoach inn, the Half-Way House. The community flourished briefly when it was rumored that a rail line was going to pass through, but when the gossip didn't pan out, Rural was destined to become the sleepy little hamlet that it is today.*

Rural is unique in Wisconsin because of its concentration of homes and buildings dating from the 1800s. The entire village has been deemed the Rural-on-the-Crystal Historic District. Historic structures are marked with plaques and include the original Half-Way House, built in 1852, which now serves as an antiques store. Rural Artists, which features the work of local craftspeople, is housed in the circa-1850 general store. Lodging is available at the Crystal River B&B (715-258-5333), an 1853 farmhouse in a pleasant setting.

19.1 Cross WI 22 and continue straight on Rural Road, one of Wisconsin's Rustic Roads.

21.0 Right onto Whispering Pines Road.

21.6 Left into Whispering Pines Park at park exit.
Whispering Pines, now affiliated with Hartman Creek State Park, began as a private park developed by three local citizens who created a lovely labyrinth of gardens and paths beneath a grove of towering cedars and white pines. The developers were a Danish couple, Christ and Emma Hyldegaard, who made their fortune in the milk business. Christ, who retired at age 42, disdained the drugs he was taking for a heart problem and decided to heal himself with fresh air and hard work. With the assistance of a friend, Casey Nowicke, he spent endless hours landscaping and building fences and stairways. The property has 2,876 feet of frontage on three different lakes. It was willed to the state when Emma Hyldegaard died in 1975.

A solid rock stairway leads to a swimming dock on Marl Lake, named for the soft white substance on the lake's bottom that gives it a translucent, blue-green color. Marl is a mixture of limestone (calcium carbonate), clay, sand, and organic deposits. The limestone is extracted from alkaline spring water by aquatic plants and by snails, which use the substance to form shells. An effective antidote to soil acidity, marl was once dredged from the lakes for use as a fertilizer.

21.8 Right onto Whispering Pines Road from the park.

22.4 Right onto Rural Road.

23.2 Left onto Hartman Creek Road.

23.8 Return to the ranger station.

If you've worked up an appetite, the Wheelhouse on County Highway Q serves great pizza. Also popular is Clearwater Harbor on County Highway QQ in the nearby village of King, which has tables on an outdoor deck overlooking Taylor Lake. Stern-wheeler excursion boats also depart from here; call 715-258-2866 for schedule and price information. A large selection of homemade pies is available at The King's Table, also on County Highway QQ.

Bicycle Repair Service

Wild Rose Bike Shop, 840 Oakwood Street, Wild Rose; 920-622-3638

The Hostel Shoppe, 929 Main Street, Stevens Point; 715-341-4340 or 1-800-233-4340

11

Waupaca/Scandinavia/Iola

- **DISTANCE:** 21.7 or 31.7 miles
- **TERRAIN:** Gently rolling

For those who fear that America will soon become a wall-to-wall shopping mall, there is hope in Waupaca. With its old-fashioned movie theater marquee, wrought-iron light posts, colorful awnings, and variety of shops and businesses, this small Wisconsin city wins our vote for "best downtown." With support of the Main Street USA program, civic-minded business owners have rallied to save their commercial district from the demise that affects many small towns.

Look for a white circular bandstand located in front of the public library at one end of Main Street. Former President Ronald Reagan delivered a nationally broadcast speech here in 1980. His whistle-stop visit was well deserved—Waupaca County ranks, per capita, as the most Republican county in the nation. At the other end of downtown is the historic Danes' Home, a major social center from 1871 to 1945. The building was built by the Danish Brotherhood, but it was used by the entire community for dances, graduations, and other events. The building now houses antiques vendors.

While the area is known for its Scandinavian heritage, the first settlers here were a group of New Englanders known as the "five Yankees from Vermont." They camped on the site of the Danes' Home and made their way to Waupaca Falls, just north of town

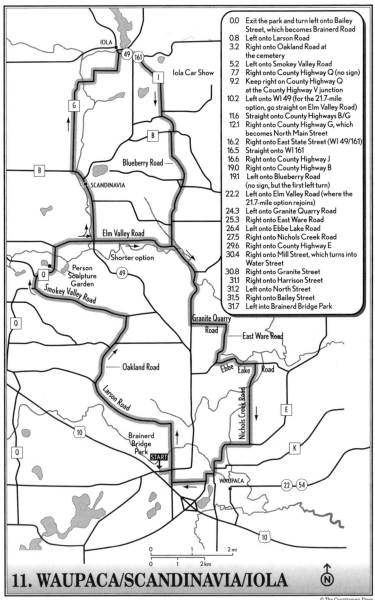

0.0	Exit the park and turn left onto Bailey Street, which becomes Brainerd Road
0.8	Left onto Larson Road
3.2	Right onto Oakland Road at the cemetery
5.2	Left onto Smokey Valley Road
7.7	Right onto County Highway Q (no sign)
9.2	Keep right on County Highway Q at the County Highway V junction
10.2	Left onto WI 49 (for the 21.7-mile option, go straight on Elm Valley Road)
11.6	Straight onto County Highways B/G
12.1	Right onto County Highway G, which becomes North Main Street
16.2	Right onto East State Street (WI 49/161)
16.5	Straight onto WI 161
16.6	Right onto County Highway J
19.0	Right onto County Highway B
19.1	Left onto Blueberry Road (no sign, but the first left turn)
22.2	Left onto Elm Valley Road (where the 21.7-mile option rejoins)
24.3	Left onto Granite Quarry Road
25.3	Right onto East Ware Road
26.4	Left onto Ebbe Lake Road
27.5	Right onto Nichols Creek Road
29.6	Right onto County Highway E
30.4	Right onto Mill Street, which turns into Water Street
30.8	Right onto Granite Street
31.1	Right onto Harrison Street
31.2	Right onto North Street
31.5	Right onto Bailey Street
31.7	Left into Brainerd Bridge Park

IOLA

Iola Car Show

Blueberry Road

SCANDINAVIA

Elm Valley Road

Shorter option

Person Sculpture Garden

Smokey Valley Road

Granite Quarry Road

East Ware Road

Oakland Road

Ebbe Lake Road

Nichols Creek Road

Larson Road

Brainerd Bridge Park

START

WAUPACA

0   1   2 mi

0   1   2 km

11. WAUPACA/SCANDINAVIA/IOLA

on the Waupaca River, where they established a sawmill. With the arrival of the Wisconsin Central Railroad in 1871, potatoes became the starch that held the economy together. Waupaca County potatoes were shipped throughout the world. At one time, Waupaca County set the international price for potatoes. The impressive home of "Potato King" A. M. Penney, located at 404 S. Main Street, was said to be the model for the Bates mansion in the Hitchcock movie *Psycho*.

If you're riding this route during the second week of July, don't be surprised if you're passed by a Model A or a '57 Chevy. The population of Iola, normally about 1,200, swells to 140,000 people when this small town hosts the annual Old Car Show. The three-day event draws vintage car aficionados from across the country who display, buy, sell, swap, and talk cars. There is a campground at the car show site, which is adjacent to Krause Publications, a major publisher of hobby magazines. Stop in if you're interested; sample publications are free to the public. Like Iola, the population of Scandinavia is principally Norwegian. This small community sponsors a number of small town summer festivals, including a free corn roast and polka fest.

This tour starts at the Brainerd Bridge Park in Waupaca. To get to the park, follow WI 10 to the Waupaca exit. Exit on Business WI 54/49 (Fulton Street) at the Baymont Motel. Turn left onto Harrison Street (WI 49) toward Iola. Turn left onto North Street and right onto Bailey Street. Follow Bailey Street to Brainerd Bridge Park, just before the Waupaca River. There is ample parking, a picnic shelter, water, and rest rooms.

0.0 Exit the park and turn left onto Bailey Street.

0.1 Keep left on Bailey Street as it turns into Brainerd Road.

0.4 Swan Park is on the left.
There are rest rooms and a picnic shelter here. This is an alternative starting point.

0.8 Left onto Larson Road.

3.2 Right onto Oakland Road at the cemetery.
Be careful as you cross the railroad tracks a short way up the road.

4.2 The Royal Oak Golf Course and Campground is on your right.
Rest rooms and snacks are available.

5.2 Left onto Smokey Valley Road.

7.7 Right onto County Highway Q where Smokey Valley Road ends (no sign).

8.3 A sculpture garden and art studio run by sculptor Roger Person are on your left.
This is worth a stop.

9.2 Keep right on County Highway Q at the County Highway V junction.

10.2 This is where the shorter and longer routes split.
If you are following the shorter option, continue straight on Elm Valley Road. This rejoins the main route at the 22.2-mile mark below.

10.2 Left onto WI 49 for the longer route. (For the 21.7-mile option, go straight on Elm Valley Road and skip to mile 22.2)
This is a busy road, but it has a good shoulder.

11.2 Enter the village of Scandinavia.
If you are lucky enough to pedal into this village on the first weekend of August, you'd better be hungry. This is the weekend of the Scandinavia Free Corn Roast. All you can eat corn on the cob is served up. Also look for lefsa, other Norwegian specialties, and homemade blueberry, cherry, apple, pear, and rhubarb pies. Entertainment includes competitions between local volunteer fire departments. In one event, an empty beer keg is suspended from a 100-foot-long cable between two telephone poles, about 20 feet above the ground. Firefighters from two departments demonstrate their aptitude as they shoot streams of water at the keg and try to send it to their opponent's side—sort of a reverse tug of war.
The Tomorrow Valley Coop has snacks, sandwiches, and rest rooms.

11.6 Straight onto County Highways B/G where WI 49 turns right.

12.0 Scandinavia Memorial Park, with rest rooms and a picnic shelter.

12.1 Right onto County Highway G, which becomes North Main Street in Iola.

15.4 Enter the village of Iola.

15.8 County Highway G becomes North Main Street at the cemetery.

The flat, gently rolling terrain makes central Wisconsin ideal for all levels of cyclists.

16.2 Downtown Iola.
Iola is another small town that received assistance from the Main Street USA program. You may want to visit the attractive downtown area. Sample the homemade pies at the Crystal Café. The Veterans Memorial Park has rest rooms.

16.2 Right onto East State Street (WI 49/161).

16.5 Straight onto WI 161 where WI 49 goes right.

16.6 Right onto County Highway J.
For the next 2 miles, you'll be riding by the grounds of the Old Car Show. The signs above each section (Ford, Chevy, Packard) signify which old cars you will find there. There are also many food and souvenir vendors during Old Car Show week.

19.0 Right onto County Highway B for about 100 yards.

19.1 Left onto Blueberry Road (no sign, but the first left turn).

22.2 Left onto Elm Valley Road.
This is where the shorter route rejoins the main route.

24.3 Left onto Granite Quarry Road.

25.3 Right onto East Ware Road.

25.8 Christianson's Orchard is on the right. Stop in the fall for some fresh apple cider.

26.4 Left onto Ebbe Lake Road where Ware Road ends.

27.5 Right onto Nichols Creek Road.

29.6 Right onto County Highway E.

30.1 Enter the village of Waupaca.

30.4 Right onto Mill Street, which turns into Water Street.

30.8 Right onto Granite Street at the Danes' Home.
Although the route continues past downtown, you may want to take some time to explore the shops and restaurants on Main Street. Enjoy a cafe latte or smoothie on the back deck of the Riverview Coffee House. Local artists exhibit at the Originals Gallery. Dragon Wings has a variety of creative toys for children. If you turn left onto Main Street and follow it to the end, you will be at South Park. History buffs will enjoy a visit to the Hutchinson House Museum. There is also a swimming beach and changing rooms.

31.1 Right onto Harrison Street.

31.2 Left onto North Street.

31.5 Right onto Bailey Street.

31.7 Left into Brainerd Bridge Park.

Bicycle Repair Service

The Wild Rose Bike Shop, 840 Oakwood Avenue, Wild Rose; 920-622-3638

The Hostel Shoppe, 929 Main Street, Stevens Point; 715-341-4340 or 1-800-233-4340

12

Wild Rose/
Christmas Tree Country

- **DISTANCE:** 31.8 miles
- **TERRAIN:** Gently rolling

Just one deep breath of the pine-scented, oxygen-rich air tells you that you're in Waushara County, the Christmas tree capital of Wisconsin. The sandy, glacial outwash soil in this area, inhospitable to most crops, is perfectly suited to the 10 million pines, firs, and spruces growing here. Wisconsin ranks third nationally in Christmas tree production and in recent years provided holiday trees for the Johnson, Carter, and Bush White Houses. Most trees require 8 to 15 years to reach harvest size; frequent pruning provides steady summer employment for area young people.

Interspersed with tree plantations and natural forests are hundreds of lakes and hidden trout streams. This is a relaxed, friendly part of Wisconsin with Mayberry-like small towns untainted by tourism and populated by people who always seem to have time to chat—especially about the weather or where the fish are biting.

The Birdsong B&B (920-622-3770) on County Highway A just east of town offers pleasant lodging in a farmhouse set on 75 acres. The innkeepers have put a generous dose of TLC into their establishment, named for the indigo buntings, orioles, bluebirds, scarlet tanagers, and other birds that visit the property. The Krahl Inn Motel (920-622-5900) also offers lodging in downtown Wild Rose.

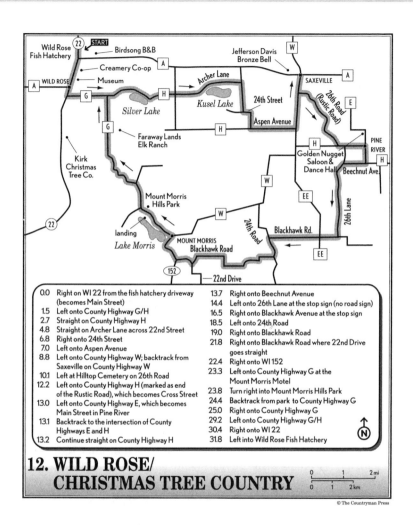

0.0	Right on WI 22 from the fish hatchery driveway (becomes Main Street)
1.5	Left onto County Highway G/H
2.7	Straight on County Highway H
4.8	Straight on Archer Lane across 22nd Street
6.8	Right onto 24th Street
7.0	Left onto Aspen Avenue
8.8	Left onto County Highway W; backtrack from Saxeville on County Highway W
10.1	Left at Hilltop Cemetery on 26th Road
12.2	Left onto County Highway H (marked as end of the Rustic Road), which becomes Cross Street
13.0	Left onto County Highway E, which becomes Main Street in Pine River
13.1	Backtrack to the intersection of County Highways E and H
13.2	Continue straight on County Highway H
13.7	Right onto Beechnut Avenue
14.4	Left onto 26th Lane at the stop sign (no road sign)
16.5	Right onto Blackhawk Avenue at the stop sign
18.5	Left onto 24th Road
19.0	Right onto Blackhawk Road
21.8	Right onto Blackhawk Road where 22nd Drive goes straight
22.4	Right onto WI 152
23.3	Left onto County Highway G at the Mount Morris Motel
23.8	Turn right into Mount Morris Hills Park
24.4	Backtrack from park to County Highway G
25.0	Right onto County Highway G
29.2	Left onto County Highway G/H
30.4	Right onto WI 22
31.8	Left into Wild Rose Fish Hatchery

12. WILD ROSE/ CHRISTMAS TREE COUNTRY

© The Countryman Press

This tour begins at the Wild Rose State Fish Hatchery (920-622-3527), ½ mile north of the village of Wild Rose on WI 22. You will find ample parking, a picnic area, and rest rooms in a park-like setting. Mileage for the ride begins at the end of the drive-way, where it meets WI 22. The hatchery has been stocking area trout streams since 1908. In addition to brown trout, the facility now raises chinook salmon, walleye, northern pike, lake sturgeon, and muskellunge—better known as the muskie. The trout area is open to the public throughout the year; northern pike and muskie cannot be viewed because of the skittishness of these species.

0.0 Right on WI 22 from the fish hatchery driveway. WI 22 becomes Main Street as you enter downtown Wild Rose.

0.6 Wild Rose Creamery Co-op is to your left.
Stop in for a favorite Wisconsin treat—a bag of cheese curds, fresh and squeaky every Friday afternoon. They also offer a nice selection of block cheeses to take home.

0.8 There are several other places of interest in the village of Wild Rose, given its name by settlers of Welsh and English descent who arrived from Rose, New York.
To your left is the Pioneer Historical Museum, which consists of several adjacent buildings, including a home furnished in the style of the 1880s, a one-room school-house, a carriage house, a smokehouse, and a blacksmith shop. Next door is the Pioneer Hall, which once housed a bank and a drug store. In a Butch Cassidy–like caper, robbers made an unsuccessful attempt to blow open the bank's vault in 1905. The head outlaw, known as Patsy, was captured, shot, and buried in the local cemetery. The museum is open Wednesday and Saturday, mid-June to Labor Day, for a small admission fee.

Early Wild Rose seemed to attract an individualist crowd. The town was home to an unusual religious sect known as the Standalones, who eschewed religious ritual and declared that every person should "stand alone and believe what he had a mind to." Today's residents are more community-minded. In an exemplary demon-stration of civic pride, Wild Rose citizens recently raised enough money to drain, dredge, and clean up the picturesque millpond that you see from Main Street. The renewed pond is the site of an annual watercross competition, where daring drivers jump snowmobiles across open water for prize money.

If you want to begin the ride with breakfast, stop in at the Chatterbox Restau-rant on your left. You can count on a bottomless cup of coffee and a free side dish of local gossip. The Vintage Garden Cafe is a personal favorite for lunch or Sunday brunch.

0.9 To your left is the old Wild Rose Mercantile Company, once a general store, now an antiques emporium with an adjoining ice cream parlor.

1.0 To your right is the Wild Rose Garden.
Though most agree the town was named after Rose, New York, the beauty of the blooming roses gives credence to an alternate explanation. The unofficial version says the town was christened when men digging the basement for the first store found a wild rose bush blooming out of season.

1.5 Left onto County Highway G/H.
Just after the turn is a grocery store; there's an ideal spot for a picnic lunch later in the ride. On your right is the first of many Christmas tree farms you will pass.

2.7 Straight on County Highway H where County Highway G turns right.

3.4 Silver Lake is to your right.

4.8 Straight on Archer Lane across 22nd Street.

5.6 Kusel Lake is to your right.

6.8 Right onto 24th Street.

7.0 Left onto Aspen Avenue.

8.8 Left onto County Highway W into Saxesville. Backtrack from Saxesville on County Highway W.

9.6 Downtown Saxeville consists of a general store that doubles as an insurance office.
Across the road from the store is a bronze bell that was once used to call the slaves from the fields at the Jefferson Davis Plantation in Corinth, Mississippi, before it was captured (or looted, depending on your viewpoint) by Saxeville soldiers in 1862.
   Backtrack out of town on County Highway W.

10.1 Left at Hilltop Cemetery on 26th Road.
This Rustic Road curves between rolling hills that typify the ground moraines found in Wisconsin's central plains region. There are several historic farms on the stretch, including the Spencer Allen Farm and the Ashcroft Farm, which also sells antiques and furniture.
   The small wooden boxes mounted on posts are bluebird houses. The bluebird population in Wisconsin has declined significantly in the last half-century due to the loss of nest sites such as hollow wooden fence posts, competition from sparrows and starlings, and the use of pesticides. Recently, bird lovers have begun to coax bluebirds back by installing nesting boxes that meet their habitat needs.

The gentle terrain is interspersed with lakes and Christmas tree farms.

12.2 Left onto County Highway H (a sign indicates the end of the Rustic Road; no other sign).
County Highway H becomes Cross Street.

13.0 Left onto County Highway E, which becomes Main Street as you enter Pine River.

13.1 To your left, with the unusual tin siding, is the Golden Nugget Saloon and Dance Hall, where local widows kick up their heels on Sunday afternoon.
There's a picnic table in a pleasant spot by the dam overlooking the Pine River. Backtrack to the intersection of County Highways E and H.

13.2 Continue straight on County Highway H at this intersection and follow it for 0.5 mile.

13.7 Right onto Beechnut Avenue, just before County Highway H makes a sharp left.

14.4 Left onto 26th Lane at the stop sign (no road sign).

16.5 Right onto Blackhawk Avenue at the stop sign.

17.0 Cross County Highway EE, still on Blackhawk Avenue.

18.5 Left onto 24th Road; follow for 0.5 mile.

19.0 Right onto Blackhawk Road.

21.8 Right onto Blackhawk Road where 22nd Drive goes straight.

22.4 Right onto WI 152 where Blackhawk Road ends.

23.2 You are entering the village of Mount Morris, which has a mill, general store, and several antiques shops.

23.3 Left onto County Highway G at the Mount Morris Motel.
Folk music concerts featuring an impressive stable of local talent are frequently held at the Mount Morris town hall on Saturday night. Call the Blackhawk Folk Society for a current schedule (920-787-7475).

23.7 To the left is the Lake Morris public landing.
This is a good spot to rest and enjoy your picnic lunch if your legs aren't up to tackling the steep climb to Mount Morris Hills Park.

23.8 If you relish a challenge, turn right into Mount Morris Hills Park.
A foot race to the top of this steep hill determined the town's name. The honor was clinched by Solomon Morris, and Gunnar Gunderson faded into oblivion.

24.4 The summit provides an awesome view of the surrounding countryside, as well as a picnic shelter and rest rooms. Backtrack from park down the hill to County Highway G.

25.0 Right onto County Highway G.

28.7 Faraway Land Elk Ranch is on the right.
Elk, called wapiti *by the Native Americans, were once native to Wisconsin. These majestic animals are raised for their meat and hides. Only the male elk have antlers, which are harvested and used for remedies in Asian natural-medicine shops.*

29.2 Left onto County Highway G/H.

30.4 Right onto WI 22.

31.8 Left into Wild Rose Fish Hatchery.

Bicycle Repair Service

Wild Rose Bike Shop, 840 Oakwood Avenue, Wild Rose; 920-622-3638

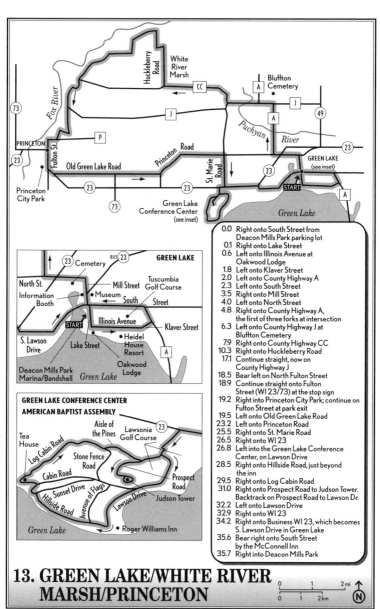

White River Marsh
Huckleberry Road
Bluffton Cemetery
Fox River
White River Marsh
73
A
CC
A
J
49
Puchyan River
P
PRINCETON
A
J
23
GREEN LAKE
(see inset)
23
23
Fulton St.
Old Green Lake Road
Princeton Road
St Marie Road
23
A
Princeton City Park
23
73
Green Lake Conference Center (see inset)
START
Green Lake

0.0	Right onto South Street from Deacon Mills Park parking lot
0.1	Right onto Lake Street
0.6	Left onto Illinois Avenue at Oakwood Lodge
1.8	Left onto Klaver Street
2.0	Left onto County Highway A
2.3	Left onto South Street
3.5	Right onto Mill Street
4.0	Left onto North Street
4.8	Right onto County Highway A, the first of three forks at intersection
6.3	Left onto County Highway J at Bluffton Cemetery
7.9	Right onto County Highway CC
10.3	Right onto Huckleberry Road
17.1	Continue straight, now on County Highway J
18.5	Bear left on North Fulton Street
18.9	Continue straight onto Fulton Street (WI 23/73) at the stop sign
19.2	Right into Princeton City Park; continue on Fulton Street at park exit
19.5	Left onto Old Green Lake Road
23.2	Left onto Princeton Road
25.5	Right onto St. Marie Road
26.5	Right onto WI 23
26.8	Left into the Green Lake Conference Center, on Lawson Drive
28.5	Right onto Hillside Road, just beyond the inn
29.5	Right onto Log Cabin Road
31.0	Right onto Prospect Road to Judson Tower. Backtrack on Prospect Road to Lawson Dr.
32.2	Left onto Lawson Drive
32.9	Right onto WI 23
34.2	Right onto Business WI 23, which becomes S. Lawson Drive in Green Lake
35.6	Bear right onto South Street by the McConnell Inn
35.7	Right into Deacon Mills Park

GREEN LAKE
23
BUS 23
Cemetery
North St.
Mill Street
Tuscumbia Golf Course
Information Booth
Museum
South Street
START
Illinois Avenue
Klaver Street
S. Lawson Drive
Lake Street
Heidel House Resort
A
Deacon Mills Park Marina/Bandshell
Oakwood Lodge
Green Lake

GREEN LAKE CONFERENCE CENTER
AMERICAN BAPTIST ASSEMBLY
Tea House
Log Cabin Road
Aisle of the Pines
Lawsonia Golf Course
23
Stone Fence Road
Cabin Road
Sunset Drive
Avenue of Flags
Prospect Road
Hillside Road
Lawson Drive
Judson Tower
Green Lake
Roger Williams Inn

13. GREEN LAKE/WHITE RIVER MARSH/PRINCETON

0   1   2 mi
0   1   2km
N

© The Countryman Press

Green Lake/ White River Marsh/ Princeton

- **DISTANCE:** 6 or 35.7 miles
- **TERRAIN:** Gently rolling

Sunlight reflecting off Green Lake's sandstone bedrock gives Wisconsin's deepest lake an emerald cast and, hence, its name. The lake fills a 7⅓-mile-long, 2-mile-wide, 237-foot-deep crater carved out by the Wisconsin Glacier. Dozens of effigy mounds in the yards of lakefront residents tell us that Winnebago Indians were the first to discover the lake's shimmering water and bountiful stock of fish.

Green Lake has a long history as a resort area, but thankfully the village has succeeded in harnessing the benefits of tourism without succumbing to flashiness. Fishing and boating dominate the local special events calendar. The Green Lake area also boasts three outstanding golf courses within a 10-mile radius—convenient if your companion prefers to be putting while you're pedaling.

Green Lake sits on Wisconsin's central plain, a region that received the full flattening effect of glacial ice. While there are enough ups and downs to keep this ride interesting, there are no real extremes. Three-fourths of Green Lake County's gently rolling prairie land is devoted to agriculture, with red barns and sky-scraping blue silos so abundant that they cease to be useful landmarks. The ride also includes cycling through White River Marsh. Biking through the marsh is not advisable during hunting season, which usually falls in early October. The Department of Natural Resources (608-266-1877) can provide the exact dates.

Families with children or those who want a shorter ride should start at the Green Lake Conference Center (mile 26.8) and do the 6-mile loop through the grounds. This is a very pleasant ride by itself, with some lovely lake views and a minimum of vehicle traffic ($1 charge per bicycle, $5 per car).

This tour begins at Deacon Mills Park next to the marina in downtown Green Lake. To get to the park, take the Business WI 23 exit from WI 23. Business WI 23 turns into South Lawson Drive as you enter town. Look for the park's old-time band shell on your right when you reach the downtown district.

0.0 Right from the parking lot of Deacon Mills Park onto South Street.
Stretch out on the cool grass, stare up at the stars, and listen to the refrains of Sondheim and Sousa when concerts are held here on Wednesday evenings in July and August. The park is also the site of a chili cook-off held annually the first weekend in September, when teams of amateur chefs compete for prizes and put on a fiery feed for the public.

0.1 Right onto Lake Street.
As you travel down Lake Street, you're heading out to Oakwood Point, where New Yorker David Greenway opened a rambling wooden frame hotel in 1867, which he touted as "the first resort west of Niagara Falls." Greenway's property included all of the land west of Lake Street and south of the Bay View Motel, totaling 3,500 acres and 2,000 feet of lakefront. The Oakwood Resort Hotel attracted well-heeled tourists from the sweltering cities of Memphis and New Orleans, where a yellow-fever epidemic was raging. In later years, Chicago and St. Louis became the main markets for Greenway's establishment, which at its peak could accommodate nearly 500 guests.

0.6 Left onto Illinois Avenue at Oakwood Lodge.
Oakwood Lodge (920-294-6580), now a bed-and-breakfast inn, was formerly the St. Louis House, the largest cottage on the Oakwood Resort Hotel property. The home immediately to the west was also one of the original cottages. The main hotel fell into disrepair and was torn down in 1929. In addition to providing overnight lodging, the inn serves bountiful country breakfasts to the public on weekends. Ask for a table on the veranda overlooking the lake.

1.2 To your right is the Heidel House Resort, and to your left Tuscumbia Golf Course.
The Heidel House is a luxurious resort, recently rebuilt after several fires. To see Green Lake from off shore, you can take a narrated cruise on the resort's 52-foot tour boat. The cruise offers great views of the impressive homes that line the lakeshore. Call for the current schedule (920-294-3344 or 1-800-444-2812). Tuscumbia, across the road, is Wisconsin's oldest golf course.

1.8 Left onto Klaver Street.

2.0 Left onto County Highway A.

2.3 Left onto South Street where County Highway A continues straight.

3.5 Right onto Mill Street through downtown Green Lake.

3.7 Just past the shopping district, you will see a millpond and dam to your left and the Dartford Historical Museum to your right.
The dam was built in 1834 by Anson Dart, founder of Dartford (later renamed Green Lake), to power his sawmill, and it is still used to control the level of Green Lake. There is a Chamber of Commerce information booth in the park that is staffed during the summer season. Opposite is the historical museum, housed in Dartford's first train station.

3.8 Continue straight onto Mill Street where Business WI 23 goes right. Look to the right before crossing. Traffic on Business WI 23 moves quickly and does not stop at this intersection.

4.0 Left onto North Street.
To your left is Dartford Cemetery, which includes the grave of one of the area's most beloved Native Americans, Chief Highknocker. The chief's name was actually Hanageh, but his habit of wearing an old top hat earned him the affectionate nickname of Highknocker. He died in 1911, and his grave is marked by a large boulder taken from an area along the lake where he liked to camp.

4.5 Cross WI 23 using caution. This is a very busy stretch and quite wide. When you reach the other side, continue straight ahead.

4.8 Right onto County Highway A. There are three forks at this intersection. County Highway A is the first one.

6.3 Left onto County Highway J at Bluffton Cemetery.

7.3 The road crosses the Puchyan River.

7.9 Right onto County Highway CC.
Just ahead on the right is a small sawmill and lumberyard. Soon after, the scenery opens up to the expansive White River Marsh, where you'll see numerous duck and goose blinds.

10.3 Right onto Huckleberry Road.
The marsh is a nesting area for sandhill cranes, which can be identified by their melancholy call and prehistoric appearance. They are large birds, averaging 3 feet in height, with an 80-inch wingspan. The best months for viewing cranes are April and October.

12.4 The road meets the Fox River.
This is a pleasant spot to pause for a few minutes. A short distance ahead on the right is a gravel road to the White River Locks Public Fishing Area. There are no services here.

17.1 Continue straight ahead where Huckleberry Road meets County Highway J. You are now traveling on County Highway J.

18.5 Bear left onto North Fulton Street where the road forks as you enter the town of Princeton.

18.9 Continue straight onto Fulton Street (also WI 23/73) at the stop sign.

19.0 If you wish to take a spin through the downtown business district, turn right onto Water Street. Otherwise, continue straight on Fulton Street.
There are a number of boutique shops and small restaurants on Water Street.

19.2 Right into Princeton City Park. Continue on Fulton Street (WI 23/73) at park exit.
Every Saturday from early May through mid-October, this is the site of Wisconsin's largest outdoor flea market. The weekly event draws antiques collectors from miles around to display their wares or to scour the city block full of tables for a rare find. There are also several antiques shops and an ice cream parlor adjacent to the park.
   Go right from the park, continuing on South Fulton Street (WI 23).

19.5 Left onto Old Green Lake Road.

23.2 Left onto Princeton Road.

25.5 Right onto St. Marie Road.

26.5 Right onto WI 23 for 0.3 mile. This is a busy road, but it has an ample paved shoulder.

26.8 Left into the Green Lake Conference Center, also known as the American Baptist Assembly (ABA) or Lawsonia. You are now on Lawson Drive.
There is a charge of $1 per bicycle, or $5 per car, for touring the grounds. The gatekeeper will give you a map (very useful if you get turned around) and a pass that you must return on your way out.

As you enter, you will be cycling through the Lawsonia Links Golf Course, opened in 1930 and considered one of the top public courses in the country. The course is laid out in the Scottish links tradition and includes unusually elevated greens with steep-faced bunkers. It is said that an old boxcar is buried beneath the seventh green. Enjoy the pleasant downhill cruise, past the boathouse and the chapel car named Grace.

The story of the Green Lake Conference Center (920-294-3323) began in 1888, when Jessie Lawson of Chicago was enjoying a pleasure-boat cruise on the lake. A sudden storm forced the captain to seek shelter at a spot called Lone Tree Point. Overwhelmed by its beauty, Mrs. Lawson convinced her husband, millionaire Chicago Daily News publisher Victor Lawson, to purchase the plot, which they developed into an impressive estate.

When Mr. Lawson died in 1925, the estate was sold to the H.O. Stone Company, which intended to build an exclusive real estate development that they touted as the "Sun Valley of the Midwest." Their plans were stalled by the Great Depression, and the property floundered with financial problems until it finally closed during World War II.

Baptist leader Dr. Luther Wesley Smith discovered the estate on a drive through Wisconsin and recognized it as a place where his dream for a national conference center could come true. In 1943, with the assistance of James L. Kraft of Kraft Foods, Dr. Smith arranged purchase of Lawsonia, valued at $11 million, for a mere $300,000. The property is still owned by the American Baptist Church and is used year-round for church-related and nondenominational conferences.

28.4 To your left is the Roger Williams Inn.
Inside this 75-room hotel you will find a snack shop and rest rooms. If you wish to climb the 113-foot Judson Tower later on this tour, pick up a key at the registration desk. In addition to the hotel, there are about 20 homes on the grounds, including

a replica of Ann Hathaway's cottage, which may be rented by families or other small groups.

28.5 Right onto Hillside Road, just beyond the inn. Continue straight on Hillside Road where Avenue of Flags goes right.
There is a narrow stone bridge here and a slight uphill. On the left is a water tower that you can climb for a great view of Green Lake.

29.0 Keep left at junctions with Sunset Drive and Cabin Road.

29.4 To your right is the Tea House.

29.5 Right onto Log Cabin Road.
Watch for deer in the large, open meadow ahead to your right, especially in the early morning or around sunset.

30.5 Stay left at the junction with Stone Fence Road. Shortly, you will pass through the Aisle of the Pines.

31.0 Right onto Prospect Road to Judson Tower. Backtrack on Prospect Road to Lawson Drive.

31.3 The road circles around Judson Tower.
It's 121 steps to the top of this water tower, which once held 75,000 gallons to supply the Lawson estate and to water the lawn with horse-drawn sprinklers. The tower is named after Adoniram Judson, a New England missionary who spent more than 30 years in Burma, where he converted many of the hill tribes to Christianity, translated the Bible into Burmese, and in 1849 completed what remains today the standard Burmese–English dictionary.

31.8 Straight on Prospect at the junction with Aisle of Pines.

32.2 Left onto Lawson Drive.

32.9 Right onto WI 23 as you exit the grounds. Take care; this is a busy road.

34.2 Right onto Business WI 23, which becomes South Lawson Drive in Green Lake.

35.4 To your right is Hattie Sherwood Park.
Here you'll find a swimming beach, picnic area, rest rooms, and a city-run campground with 34 sites, some with electricity.

35.6 Bear right onto South Street by the McConnell Inn.
This charming Victorian home built in 1901 is now operated as a bed-and-breakfast inn (920-294-6430 or 1-888-238-8625).

35.7 Right into Deacon Mills Park.

Bicycle Repair Service

Mike's Bike Shop, 117 East Huron Street, Berlin; 920-361-3565

DOOR
COUNTY

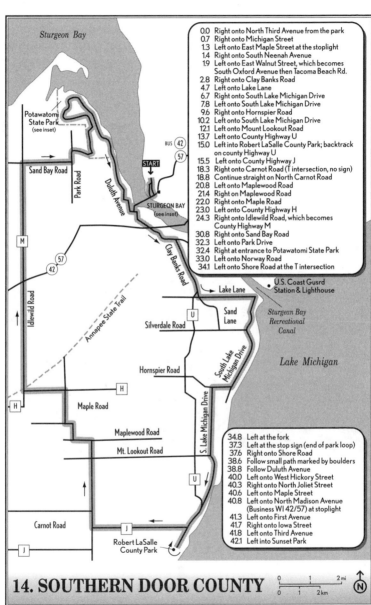

Sturgeon Bay

0.0 Right onto North Third Avenue from the park
0.7 Right onto Michigan Street
1.3 Left onto East Maple Street at the stoplight
1.4 Right onto South Neenah Avenue
1.9 Left onto East Walnut Street, which becomes
     South Oxford Avenue then Tacoma Beach Rd.
2.8 Right onto Clay Banks Road
4.7 Left onto Lake Lane
6.7 Right onto South Lake Michigan Drive
7.8 Left onto South Lake Michigan Drive
9.6 Right onto Hornspier Road
10.2 Left onto South Lake Michigan Drive
12.1 Left onto Mount Lookout Road
13.7 Left onto County Highway U
15.0 Left into Robert LaSalle County Park; backtrack
     on county Highway U
15.5 Left onto County Highway J
18.3 Right onto Carnot Road (T intersection, no sign)
18.8 Continue straight on North Carnot Road
20.8 Left onto Maplewood Road
21.4 Right on Maplewood Road
22.0 Right onto Maple Road
23.0 Left onto County Highway H
24.3 Right onto Idlewild Road, which becomes
     County Highway M
30.8 Right onto Sand Bay Road
32.3 Left onto Park Drive
32.4 Right at entrance to Potawatomi State Park
33.0 Left onto Norway Road
34.1 Left onto Shore Road at the T intersection

Potawatomi
State Park
(see inset)

BUS 42
57
START

Sand Bay Road

Park Road

Duluth Avenue

STURGEON BAY
(see inset)

M

57
42

Idlewild Road

Clay Banks Road

Annapee State Trail

Lake Lane

U.S. Coast Gusrd
Station & Lighthouse

Sand
Lane

U

*Sturgean Bay
Recreational
Canal*

Silverdale Road

South Lake Michigan Drive

Lake Michigan

Hornspier Road

H

H

Maple Road

Maplewood Road

Mt. Lookout Road

S. Lake Michigan Drive

U

Carnot Road

J

J

Robert LaSalle
County Park

34.8 Left at the fork
37.3 Left at the stop sign (end of park loop)
37.6 Right onto Shore Road
38.6 Follow small path marked by boulders
38.8 Follow Duluth Avenue
40.0 Left onto West Hickory Street
40.3 Right onto North Joliet Street
40.6 Left onto Maple Street
40.8 Left onto North Madison Avenue
     (Business WI 42/57) at stoplight
41.3 Left onto First Avenue
41.7 Right onto Iowa Street
41.8 Left onto Third Avenue
42.1 Left into Sunset Park

14. SOUTHERN DOOR COUNTY

0   1   2 mi
0   1   2 km

N

Southern Door County

- **DISTANCE:** 42.1 miles (0.75 mile of dirt road)
- **TERRAIN:** Flat to gently rolling

A friend once confessed to a passion for "anything that floats." If you share that persuasion, put this tour on your "to do" list. Boats of every description—intrepid little tugs, cavernous cargo ships, even Ted Turner's sexy yacht, *Tenacious,* have been born in Sturgeon Bay, the starting point of this tour. This unpretentious port of call is the largest shipbuilding center on the Great Lakes and home to three major shipbuilding firms. Commercial fishing, fruit growing, and limestone quarrying round out the local economy.

The rise of the shipbuilding industry began in 1866, when Congress granted 200,000 acres for the construction of the Sturgeon Bay Ship Canal. Prior to that, Native Americans, explorers, missionaries, and fur traders were forced to decide between a demanding portage across the peninsula and a treacherous voyage around its tip, through the passage known as "Death's Door." The corridor was initially large enough for only a rowboat or canoe to pass—today it's a major shipping waterway.

This tour includes one unpaved stretch of road that extends for about ¾ mile along the Lake Michigan shore. Even if you walk this portion, it's well worth it for the lake views. You may notice that the route crosses the Ahnapee Trail. This rails-to-trails project is suitable for snowmobiling and hiking only; the surface hasn't been improved for cycling.

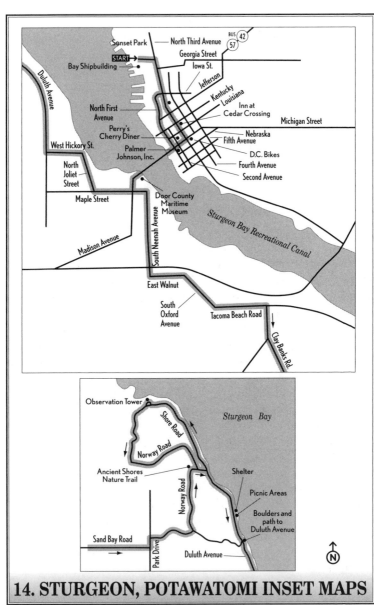

Sonset Park — North Third Avenue   BUS 57 / 42

START→   Georgia Street
Bay Shipbuilding   Iowa St.

Duluth Avenue

Jefferson

Kentucky
Louisiana

North First
Avenue   Inn at
Cedar Crossing   Michigan Street

West Hickory St.   Perry's
Cherry Diner   Nebraska
Fifth Avenue

Palmer
Johnson, Inc.   D.C. Bikes

North
Joliet
Street   Fourth Avenue
Second Avenue

Maple Street   Door County
Maritime
Museum

South Neenah Avenue   Sturgeon Bay Recreational Canal

Madison Avenue

East Walnut

South
Oxford
Avenue   Tacoma Beach Road

Clay Banks Rd.

Observation Tower   Sturgeon Bay

Shore Road

Norway Road

Ancient Shores
Nature Trail   Shelter

Norway Road   Picnic Areas

Boulders and
path to
Duluth Avenue

Sand Bay Road

Park Drive

Duluth Avenue   N

14. STURGEON, POTAWATOMI INSET MAPS

© The Countryman Press

The tour begins at Sunset Park, next to the Bay Shipbuilding Company and just north of downtown Sturgeon Bay. Follow Business WI 42/57 into Sturgeon Bay. From the north, turn right on Georgia Street. Continue for four blocks, then turn right on North Third Avenue. The park is on your left, just beyond the shipyard. From the south, cross over the Sturgeon Bay Canal and turn left on First Avenue, just beyond the bridge. Follow First Avenue until it runs into North Third Avenue. Turn left on Third Avenue and continue for several blocks. Parking, rest rooms, and picnic tables are available at the park.

0.0 Right onto North Third Avenue from the park.
To your right is the Bay Shipbuilding Company. Facilities include a 7,000-ton floating dry dock and the largest gantry crane in the world. Great Lakes and ocean-going freighters are built and maintained here. Visitors are not allowed in the dock area, but the enormous scale of the shipyard's projects makes it easy to observe from the road.

0.6 The Inn at Cedar Crossing (920-743-4200) is to your left at the junction with Louisiana Street.
Innkeeper Teri Smith has transformed this turn-of-the-20th-century vernacular brick building into a popular restaurant, pub, bakery, and bed-and-breakfast inn.

If you've forgotten an essential cycling accessory or are in need of repairs, Door County Bicycle Works, or D.C. Bikes (920-743-4434), a bicycle and outdoor apparel shop, is located at 20 North Third Avenue, a few blocks south of the inn.

0.7 Right onto Michigan Street.
Look for Perry's Cherry Diner with the red-striped awning on your right shortly after the turn, and you'll find a darling little restaurant with a '50s theme. Perry's features awesome homemade malts and a "waffle made in heaven, right here on earth." Another plus for cyclists—Perry's is a nonsmoking diner.

On your left, just before the bridge over the Sturgeon Bay Canal, is Palmer Johnson, Inc., which has been building boats at this location since 1918. Through the years, the company has produced fishing vessels, air-sea rescue boats, freighters, custom sailboats, and world-class racing yachts. The "who's who" of Palmer Johnson boat owners includes King Juan Carlos of Spain, who owns a 100-foot motor yacht named Fortuna. Several blocks away is Peterson Builders, Inc., whose ship-building vita includes Seaprobe, Alcoa's ocean research vessel, the

world's largest tuna-fishing boat, Navy minesweepers, and Alaskan ferries.
Caution: *As you cross, use the walking bridge to the left of car lanes.*

Just over the bridge is the Door County Maritime Museum. Highlights include the pilothouse from the steamship Elba, *a 1902 Chris-Craft speedboat, an extensive lighthouse exhibit, a working periscope, and a replica of the office of Captain John Roen, who was known for his ingenuity in solving challenging salvage problems.*

One notable feat was his 1943 Houdini-like resurrection of the George M. Humphrey, *a 586-foot steamer carrying 14,000 gross tons of iron ore that sank off Michigan's Mackinac Island. Because the wreck posed a danger to passing ferries, the United States War Department sought bids to destroy it with dynamite. Enter Captain John Roen, who offered to remove the boat within one year, if he could claim ownership upon completion of the task. Roen made history by filling the ship's ballast tanks with air and using the buoyancy of the water to lift the Humphrey to the surface.*

1.3 Left onto East Maple Street at the stoplight.

1.4 Right onto South Neenah Avenue.

1.8 Cross WI 42/57. Be careful, traffic is heavy here.

1.9 Left onto East Walnut Street.

2.1 Cross Shiloh Road. East Walnut Street becomes South Oxford Avenue.

2.5 South Oxford Avenue becomes Tacoma Beach Road.

2.8 Right onto Clay Banks Road.

4.7 Left onto Lake Lane.
Watch for deer on this lovely stretch of birch-lined road.

6.7 Right onto South Lake Michigan Drive.
Walk to the shore to see the Lake Michigan entrance to the Sturgeon Bay Recreational Canal, guarded by a picturesque lighthouse and Coast Guard station.

7.8 Left onto South Lake Michigan Drive at the junction with Silverdale Road.

8.9 An unpaved stretch begins here, lasting about 0.75 mile.

9.6 Right onto Hornspier Road.

Rolling along the Lake Michigan shore

10.2 Left onto South Lake Michigan Drive.

12.1 Left onto Mount Lookout Road.

13.7 Left onto County Highway U.

14.1 Pass Lower LaSalle County Park and Braunsdorf Beach.

15.0 Left into Robert LaSalle County Park.
Look for a parking area and small sign. Be sure to walk down the hill to the quiet, secluded beach where you will find rest rooms and picnic tables.
   Go right onto County Highway U, and backtrack to County Highway J.

15.5 Left onto County Highway J.

18.3 Right onto Carnot Road (no sign) where County Highway J goes left (T intersection).

18.8 Continue straight on North Carnot Road at Carnot Corners. Don't take the branch of Carnot Road that goes left.

20.8 Left onto Maplewood Road where Carnot Road ends.

21.4 Right on Maplewood Road.

22.0 Right onto Maple Road.

23.0 Left onto County Highway H (road sign is behind stop sign).
Most of Door County's famous Red Tart (Mortmorency) cherries are grown in this area. These are baking cherries and are quite sour if eaten uncooked. For snacking, try dried cherries—Wisconsin's counterpart to California raisins. Apple varieties grown in Door County include Delicious, McIntosh, Cortlands, Greenings, and Snows. White apple blossoms open in mid-May, followed by pink cherry blossoms a week or so later. If Mother Nature cooperates, both are in full bloom for Memorial Day weekend.

24.3 Right onto Idlewild Road where County Highway H goes left.

27.1 Cross WI 42/57. Use caution, this is a busy road.
Idlewild Road becomes County Highway M here.

30.8 Right onto Sand Bay Road.

32.3 Left onto Park Drive.

32.4 Right at entrance to Potawatomi State Park.
The park sits on the edge of the Niagara Escarpment, a 900-mile-long slab of dolomite limestone that extends from New York, where it supports the plunging waters of Niagara Falls. Pileated woodpeckers are numerous in the park. Look for a large bird that resembles the cartoon character named Woody, often spotted in places where field meets forest. You may notice large oblong holes in the red pines; these are made by woodpeckers looking for ants and beetles.

33.0 Left onto Norway Road toward the tower.

34.1 Left onto Shore Road at the T intersection.

34.8 Take the left fork and continue uphill to the tower.
Gear down, it's a big climb.

35.4 Climb the 75-foot observation tower for a view of Marinette, Wisconsin, and Menominee, Michigan, 16 miles across the bay. There are rest rooms here.

37.3 Left at the stop sign (end of park loop).

37.6 Right onto Shore Road.

38.6 Look for several boulders marking a small path. Follow the path for 0.2 mile where it meets Duluth Avenue.

38.8 Follow Duluth Avenue back to Sturgeon Bay.

40.0 Left onto West Hickory Street.

40.3 Right onto North Joliet Street.

40.6 Left onto Maple Street.

40.8 Left onto North Madison Avenue (Business WI 42/57) at stoplight. Cross the Sturgeon Bay Canal using the walking bridge on the right side.

41.3 Left onto First Avenue.

41.7 Right onto Iowa Street.

41.8 Left onto Third Avenue.

42.1 Left into Sunset Park.

Bicycle Repair Service

Door County Bicycle Works (D.C. Bikes), 20 North Third Avenue, Sturgeon Bay; 920-743-4434

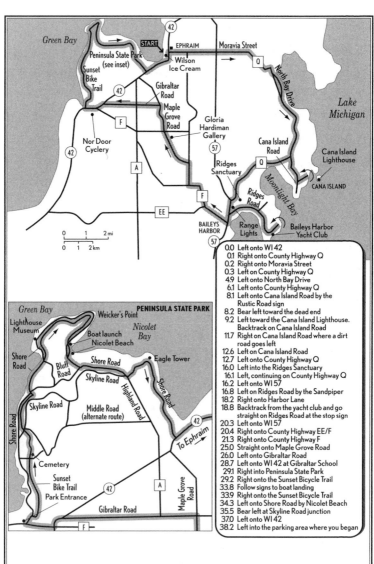

0.0	Left onto WI 42
0.1	Right onto County Highway Q
0.2	Right onto Moravia Street
0.3	Left on County Highway Q
4.9	Left onto North Bay Drive
6.1	Left onto County Highway Q
8.1	Left onto Cana Island Road by the Rustic Road sign
8.2	Bear left toward the dead end
9.2	Left toward the Cana Island Lighthouse. Backtrack on Cana Island Road
11.7	Right on Cana Island Road where a dirt road goes left
12.6	Left on Cana Island Road
12.7	Left onto County Highway Q
16.0	Left into the Ridges Sanctuary
16.1	Left, continuing on County Highway Q
16.2	Left onto WI 57
16.8	Left on Ridges Road by the Sandpiper
18.2	Right onto Harbor Lane
18.8	Backtrack from the yacht club and go straight on Ridges Road at the stop sign
20.3	Left onto WI 57
20.4	Right onto County Highway EE/F
21.3	Right onto County Highway F
25.0	Straight onto Maple Grove Road
26.0	Left onto Gibraltar Road
28.7	Left onto WI 42 at Gibraltar School
29.1	Right into Peninsula State Park
29.2	Right onto the Sunset Bicycle Trail
33.8	Follow signs to boat landing
33.9	Right onto the Sunset Bicycle Trail
34.3	Left onto Shore Road by Nicolet Beach
35.5	Bear left at Skyline Road junction
37.0	Left onto WI 42
38.2	Left into the parking area where you began

15. EPHRAIM/BAILEYS HARBOR/ PENINSULA STATE PARK

© The Countryman Press

Ephraim/Baileys Harbor/ Peninsula State Park

- **DISTANCE:** 11.9 or 38.2 miles (5.2 miles of unpaved surface)
- **TERRAIN:** Gently rolling

Welcome to postcard Door County—neatly whitewashed waterfront villages, lighthouses surrounded by swooping gulls, and sailboats bobbing in the harbor, their rigging clanging like soprano wind chimes. On this ride you will meet the contrasting personalities of both the Green Bay and Lake Michigan shores—the bay side a hub of friendly activity, the lake side given to solitude and introspection.

Across the bay from the tour starting point in Ephraim is the 3,763-acre, densely wooded peninsula that makes up Peninsula State Park. This view varies with constantly changing weather and light conditions—gray and storm-beaten during a full-force gale, barely visible behind a lace curtain of morning mist, or backlit by a rosy-peach sunset—an appropriate study for a modern-day Monet.

If you plan to cycle this route on a weekend in July or August, don't be discouraged when you arrive in Ephraim to find backed-up traffic and a shortage of parking spots. Take solace in the fact that this ride follows lightly traveled back roads and seldom crosses the main thoroughfares.

The terrain is flat to rolling with the exception of two formidable hills—one near the start of the ride and another in Peninsula State Park. Those looking for a shorter, more leisurely option should consider cycling just the 11.9-mile portion in Peninsula State Park, which follows the level, off-road Sunset Bicycle Trail. Skip to mile 29.1 for directions. The trail surface is a firm, crushed limestone, suitable for all except the thinnest racing tires. Parking and a map are available at the park office.

Cyclists wishing to camp in Peninsula State Park should call ahead for reservations (920-868-3258); holiday weekends fill early. Hotel and bed-and-breakfast accommodations are plentiful in the area; contact the Door County Chamber of Commerce (414-743-4456). The Chamber also publishes a bicycle map for Door County, and bike route signs along the roads indicate the loop that has been laid out. Be aware that these signs do not always correspond to this route. In fact, you will sometimes need to turn in the opposite direction.

WI 42 will take you to the village of Ephraim. The tour begins at the municipal parking lot opposite Wilson's Restaurant and the Ephraim Public Library.

0.0 Left onto WI 42.

0.1 Right onto County Highway Q.

0.2 Right onto Moravia Street (also County Highway Q).
Pause here for a moment to muster your energy for the big hill ahead. On your left is a pioneer schoolhouse that served Ephraim for 80 years. Ahead, in the next block, you can see the Ephraim Moravian Church, identified by its white steeple and green shutters.

Ephraim was founded in 1853 by members of the Norwegian Moravian Church under the leadership of the Reverend Andreas M. Iverson. The Moravians formed earlier settlements in Milwaukee and Green Bay, but they disbanded because of dissatisfaction with the philosophy of collective ownership espoused by their leader, Nils Otto Tank. When they arrived in Door County, they called their new settlement Ephraim, a word that appears frequently in the Bible and means "doubly fruitful." The strict moral standards of the Moravian community remain today—liquor sales are still forbidden in the village.

0.3 Left on County Highway Q and proceed up the hill.
Don't be discouraged by this steep climb. Once you reach the top, you will be riding on a vast plateau of Niagara limestone that stretches the length of the peninsula.

2.1 Cross WI 57. Use caution, this is a busy road.

4.9 Left onto North Bay Drive.
This short diversion off County Highway Q takes you down to the water's edge.

6.1 Left onto County Highway Q again.

8.1 Left by the Rustic Road sign onto Cana Island Road.

8.2 Bear left toward the dead end (don't turn right); follow the Rustic Road sign.
This road passes between Moonlight Bay and North Bay, through a boreal forest filled with magnificent specimens of spruce, cedar, and white pine. These trees are more typical of vegetation found in northern Minnesota or Canada, but because of the cooling effect of Lake Michigan they are able to grow here.

9.2 Left toward the Cana Island Lighthouse (still on Rustic Road), where the road ahead becomes dirt.

10.5 Park your bike where the road ends and walk across the isthmus to the lighthouse.
For a small fee, you may tour the lighthouse building (but not the tower) from 10 AM to 5 PM daily. When you return to the mainland, backtrack on Cana Island Road.

11.7 Right on Cana Island Road where a dirt road goes left.

12.6 Left on Cana Island Road.

12.7 Left onto County Highway Q.

16.0 Left into the Ridges Sanctuary (920-839-2802).
The sanctuary features hiking trails that follow the crests (or ridges) of ancient Lake Michigan shorelines, created as waters rose and fell through the centuries. The sandy soil here and the swales that form in the troughs between the ridges create a unique habitat for wildflowers and other forest plants. More than 20 species of native orchids bloom in the sanctuary. A self-guided hike takes about an hour; naturalists lead interpretive walks during the summer months. Bring insect repellent!

16.1 Left, continuing on County Highway Q as you leave the sanctuary.

16.2 Left onto WI 57.

The village of Ephraim on Green Bay

16.5 Enter the village of Baileys Harbor.
In the late 1840s, Captain Justice Bailey took refuge from a storm in the pictur-esque harbor that now bears his name. He was headed from Milwaukee to Buffalo with a boatload of immigrants in search of a new home. Bailey was impressed with the ample supplies of timber and limestone and convinced the owner of his schooner to purchase land and form a settlement here. Baileys Harbor later became a regular refueling stop on the steamship line between Chicago and Buffalo.

16.8 Left on Ridges Road by the Sandpiper Restaurant.

17.0 To the left are two range lights, used to guide ships into the harbor.
The lights were built in 1869, as part of an effort by the federal government to put an end to Door County's history of tragic shipwrecks. The upper range light, also the keeper's home, is located 950 feet inland from the lower light and stands 17 feet higher. Ship captains lined up the towers during the day, or the beacons that shone in them at night, to guide their vessels into port. The lamps were fueled by lard, whale oil, and kerosene before being converted to electricity in the 1930s. The range lights were used until 1969, when the single automated light was installed across the road.

17.1 Baileys Harbor Ridges County Park, on your right just past the range lights, has rest rooms and a nice beach.

18.2 Right onto Harbor Lane toward the Baileys Harbor Yacht Club.

18.5 When you reach the yacht club, walk down to the pier and admire the many sailing and motor yachts moored here.

18.8 Backtrack from the yacht club and go straight on Ridges Road at the stop sign.

20.3 Left onto WI 57.

20.4 Right onto County Highway EE/F, just beyond the McArdle Library and Tourist Information Office. There is a small park with a picnic shelter here. Rest rooms are available inside the library.

21.3 Right onto County Highway F at the stop sign.

25.0 Straight onto Maple Grove Road (not right onto Maple Grove East). *The Gloria Hardiman Gallery at this intersection specializes in hand-woven woolen goods.*

26.0 Left onto Gibraltar Road.

27.0 Cross County Highway A.

28.7 Left onto WI 42 at Gibraltar School. The road is busy, but there is an ample paved shoulder.

29.0 To your left is Nor Door Cyclery, a friendly, full-service bicycle shop.

29.1 Right into Peninsula State Park. (The short, in-park loop begins here.) *Our route through the park will include some stretches on the Sunset Bike Trail and others on the road. There are no entrance or trail fees for cyclists. If you prefer not to ride on an unpaved surface, you can take the Shore Road through the park, but there is a great deal of camper traffic during the summer.*

29.2 Right onto the Sunset Bicycle Trail, just past the entrance.

30.4 Cross the road by the cemetery.

31.7 To your left is the Eagle Lighthouse and Museum. *The lighthouse was built in 1868 in the interest of maritime safety. The museum is*

*open to visitors from June through Labor Day for a small admission fee. From the
museum, continue on the Sunset Bicycle Trail.*

33.3 Welkers Point Picnic Area, on your left, makes a good lunch stop.

33.8 Follow signs down to the boat landing and Nicolet Bay campsites
#600–677.

33.9 Right again onto the Sunset Bicycle Trail.

34.2 The trail leads to Nicolet Beach, with a sandy area for swimming, a picnic area, and rest rooms.
*It is named for Jean Nicolet, who arrived in Door County in 1634 dressed in a
mandarin robe, in preparation for his arrival in China.
   Backtrack to the exit and turn left onto Shore Road.*

34.3 Left onto Shore Road toward Eagle Tower.
Get ready for the second big hill of the ride.

35.5 Bear left at Skyline Road junction.

35.7 Eagle Bluff Lookout and the 75-foot Eagle Tower.
*Both offer stunning views of the Green Bay shoreline, including Chambers, Horse-
shoe, Little Strawberry, Pirate, Jack, and Adventure Islands. From the tower, it's all
downhill back to Ephraim. As you coast past the park's golf course, notice the 40-
foot totem pole on your left, topped with a carved bear, clan symbol of the
Potawatomi tribe. The pole marks the grave of Chief Simon Kahquados.
   To complete the in-park loop, backtrack from Eagle Tower and take Highland
Road to Middle Road. Middle Road is almost entirely downhill. Beware, the last
section is very steep, and there is a sharp left at the bottom of the hill. Turn left onto
Mengelberg Lane and take another left onto the Sunset Bike Trail to get back to
the parking lot.*

37.0 Left onto WI 42. This is a busy road, but it has a shoulder for cyclists.

38.2 Left into the parking area where you began.
*An ice cream cone from Wilson's is a Door County must-do—a jelly bean is cleverly
included in the bottom of your cone to prevent dripping.*

Bicycle Repair Service

Nor Door Cyclery, 4007 WI 42, Fish Creek; 920-868-2275

16

Ellison Bay/Gills Rock/ Newport State Park

- **DISTANCE:** 19.2 miles
- **TERRAIN:** Flat to gently rolling

Door County's tranquil "top of the thumb" area is a world apart from the bustling villages farther south on the peninsula. While you'll come across the occasional pottery shop or ice cream parlor, the attractions here are natural rather than commercial.

The water is never far away on this short ride that takes in both the Green Bay and Lake Michigan shores and the turbulent channel known as Death's Door. On a foggy morning, with only a gentle stretch of the imagination, you'd think you were on the coast of Oregon or Maine. With the exception of one hill, which is steep enough to be a "walker" for most, the terrain is flat and the traffic light to nonexistent. Most visitors who make it this far north are headed for the ferry to Washington Island, but if you have an afternoon to spare, there's plenty worth exploring before you pull anchor. For those with the inclination to do both, the Washington Island ride can easily be combined with this one.

The tour begins at the Women's Club Park, located just south of Ellison Bay on WI 42. If you're traveling north from Sister Bay, be sure to stop at the Grand View Motel, just south of Ellison Bay, for a panoramic view of Green Bay and offshore islands. As you descend a large hill from the motel, Women's Club Park is on your left.

0.0 Left on WI 42, leaving the park.

Ellison Bay was founded in 1872 by Danish immigrant John Eliason, a local timber

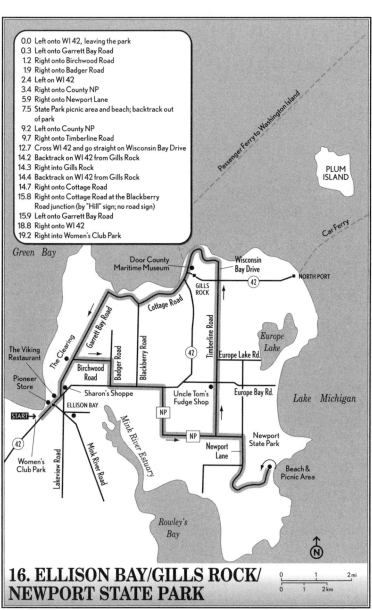

0.0 Left onto WI 42, leaving the park
0.3 Left onto Garrett Bay Road
1.2 Right onto Birchwood Road
1.9 Right onto Badger Road
2.4 Left on WI 42
3.4 Right onto County NP
5.9 Right onto Newport Lane
7.5 State Park picnic area and beach; backtrack out
      of park
9.2 Left onto County NP
9.7 Right onto Timberline Road
12.7 Cross WI 42 and go straight on Wisconsin Bay Drive
14.2 Backtrack on WI 42 from Gills Rock
14.3 Right into Gills Rock
14.4 Backtrack on WI 42 from Gills Rock
14.7 Right onto Cottage Road
15.8 Right onto Cottage Road at the Blackberry
      Road junction (by "Hill" sign; no road sign)
15.9 Left onto Garrett Bay Road
18.8 Right onto WI 42
19.2 Right into Women's Club Park

Passenger Ferry to Washington Island

PLUM
ISLAND

Car Ferry

Green Bay

Door County
Maritime Museum

Wisconsin
Bay Drive

GILLS
ROCK

NORTH PORT

42

Cottage Road

Garrett Bay Road

The Clearing

Europe
Lake

Timberline Road

42

Europe Lake Rd.

The Viking
Restaurant

Badger Road

Blackberry Road

Birchwood
Road

Europe Bay Rd.

Lake Michigan

Pioneer
Store

Sharon's Shoppe

Uncle Tom's
Fudge Shop

START

ELLISON BAY

NP

Newport
State Park

42

NP

Newport
Lane

Beach &
Picnic Area

Women's
Club Park

Lakeview Road

Mink River Road

Mink River Estuary

Rowley's
Bay

N

16. ELLISON BAY/GILLS ROCK/
NEWPORT STATE PARK

0   1   2 mi

0   1   2 km

baron who made his fortune in the telephone-pole business. The Pioneer Store, on your left, is a good spot to stock up on provisions for your ride. Built in 1900, this old-time general store epitomizes the axiom, "If they don't have it, you don't need it." Besides buying comestibles, you can drop off your dry cleaning here, and if you need his services, the grocer is a notary public. The Hotel Disgarden (920-854-9888) is a historic seven-room bed-and-breakfast inn with the village at its front door and the local marina in back.

Just ahead on the left is the Viking Restaurant, home of Door County's longest running fish boil. Inquire about dinner seating times when you pass by—this is a great place to satisfy a cyclist's post-ride appetite. The fish boil became a Door County tradition in turn-of-the-20th-century lumber camps, where local whitefish provided an inexpensive yet filling meal for the lumberjacks. The camp cook tossed potatoes, onions, large chunks of whitefish, and, in those days, enormous quantities of salt into a huge kettle over a raging bonfire. When all the ingredients were cooked, wood was added to the fire, causing the kettle to boil over. Along with the foamy water that spewed forth went the strong, "fishy" taste associated with this rather rough fish. The "boil over" remains the grand finale and prime photo opportunity of the present-day fish boil.

0.3 Left on Garrett Bay Road by the old Gus Klenke garage.
Just beyond the garage is Sharon's Shoppe, where you can cure your ice cream craving. Ahead and to your left on Garrett Bay Road is The Clearing (920-854-4088), originally the summer home of Jens Jensen, the prominent American landscape architect. According to Jensen, the word clearing refers to a clearing of the mind. He built the home as a place where his students could "withdraw from the manmade world." Today, The Clearing is a school where students pursue writing and artistic endeavors in an inspirational natural setting. Tours are available on Saturday and Sunday afternoons during the summer months.

1.2 Right onto Birchwood Road.

1.9 Right onto Badger Road.
Here you'll pass apple and cherry orchards, some regrettably abandoned in recent years.

2.4 Left and follow WI 42 for about 1 mile.
This is a busy road, so stay in single file. Along this stretch look for roadside stands and orchard stores selling apples, cider, and homemade preserves, especially in the fall.

Fall colors in Newport State Park, an undiscovered corner of Door County

3.4 Right onto County NP.

5.9 Right onto Newport Lane.

6.4 Enter Newport State Park and continue on Newport Lane.
There is no entry fee for bicycles, but you may want to pick up a park map at the entry gate. Because the campsites here can only be reached by backpacking,

Newport State Park draws fewer visitors than other Door County parks. The park was a logging village in the 1800s. Old dock cribs, lilac hedges, and a few remains of cabin foundations can still be found here.

7.5 Newport Lane ends at parking area #3.
Here you will find a beautiful sandy beach that extends for several miles. There are changing facilities if you dare to take a polar-bear dip in Lake Michigan. For the not-so-daring, beachcombing nets all sorts of unusual treasures. Those with mountain bikes can try out a new off-road bicycle trail through the park. Signs point to the trail from the beach area.

Backtrack out of the park on Newport Lane.

9.2 Left onto County NP.

9.7 Right onto Timberline Road (your first right, opposite Century Farm).

10.7 Uncle Tom's Fudge Shop is on your left, opposite Europe Bay Road.
This little blue Newport Schoolhouse, dating to 1858, is where Uncle Tom, unofficially known as "the Socrates of Door County," peddled his own brand of pancake mix, peanut brittle, fudge, and homespun philosophy until he died in 1991. Among Tom's favorite customers were cyclists, who often spent hours warming up around his pot-bellied stove and listening to his snippets of wisdom like "gratitude is attitude." The walls of the store are papered with photos of Uncle Tom with friends, politicians, and celebrities. The store is still in operation and makes an interesting snack stop.

12.7 Cross WI 42 and go straight on Wisconsin Bay Drive.
This road winds along a rugged bluff past some of Door County's most beautiful homes, including that of well-known watercolorist Tom Lynch.

14.1 Just as you enter the village of Gills Rock, the Door County Maritime Museum is on your left.
Exhibits at the museum (920-854-1844) focus on the area's commercial fishing industry and include a 60-year-old refurbished commercial fishing tug called Hope*. The museum has rest rooms.*

14.2 Right onto WI 42.

14.3 Right into Gills Rock where WI 42 goes left.
Gregarious gulls will greet you as you arrive at Gills Rock, where the Shoreline Resort offers harborside rooms (920-854-2606). Both commercial and sport

fishing boats depart from here, and if you arrive in midafternoon, you are likely to see them coming in with the day's catch. Near the dock are several souvenir shops and Charlie's Smokehouse, where you can buy a piece of delicious smoked white-fish. This gourmet delight travels well in a handlebar bag, or it can be enjoyed pier-side with rye crackers and a cold drink.

From Gills Rock you can catch a glimpse of the treacherous passage between the Door Peninsula and Washington Island that the French explorers called Porte des Morts (Death's Door). Strong variable currents make the coastal waters here tricky to navigate, particularly during winter storms. Between 1837 and 1914, 24 vessels were lost in the Porte des Morts, and another 40 boats ran aground on nearby reefs, shoals, and islands. The two passenger ferry lines that now service Washington Island from Gills Rock have a much better safety record.

Backtrack from Gills Rock on WI 42.

14.4 Backtrack on WI 42 from Gills Rock.

14.7 Right onto Cottage Road.
This road traces a craggy shoreline, then turns inland to a deep boreal forest.

15.8 Right again onto Cottage Road at the Blackberry Road junction, by the "Hill" sign (no road signs here).
Luckily, the sign indicates a downhill, but be aware that the hill is very steep and there is often loose gravel at the edges of the road. Anticipate a sharp, 90-degree turn at the bottom.

15.9 Left at the hill bottom onto Garrett Bay Road.
From here it's a pleasant coast back to Ellison Bay under a canopy of massive maples. This stretch is especially delightful in mid-May, when delicate white trillium blossoms poke their noses out among the tree trunks. As you approach the high-way, it's your last chance for ice cream.

18.8 Right onto WI 42.

19.2 Right into Women's Club Park.

Bicycle Repair Service

Nor Door Cyclery, 4007 WI 42, Fish Creek; 920-868-2275

17

Washington Island

- **DISTANCE:** 24.3 miles
- **TERRAIN:** Flat to rolling

While Washington Island's isolated locale may have discouraged less intrepid immigrants, the hearty Icelandic settlers who arrived here in the mid-1800s felt right at home. Today, the island has a population of about 650 permanent residents who earn their living from tourism, commercial fishing, and various artistic endeavors. Washington Island remains the oldest, and one of the largest, Icelandic communities outside of Reykjavik. The island was called Potawatomi Island for its resident tribe until 1816, when a Navy fleet stranded here renamed it Washington Island in honor of its flagship.

A complete circumnavigation of the island is only 24 miles, making a bicycle the ideal way to explore. Those hungry for more mileage can easily combine this ride with the northern Door County route.

Two ferry companies provide service to Washington Island, and both allow you to bring your bike on board. The most comfortable way to travel is on the upper deck of the passenger-only Island Clipper (920-854-2972), which departs from Gills Rock. Captain Charlie Voight gives a brief commentary along the way. A car ferry, operated by the Washington Island Ferry Line, departs from Northport (920-847-2546). This boat operates earlier and later in the season and is also more likely to go in inclement weather. The

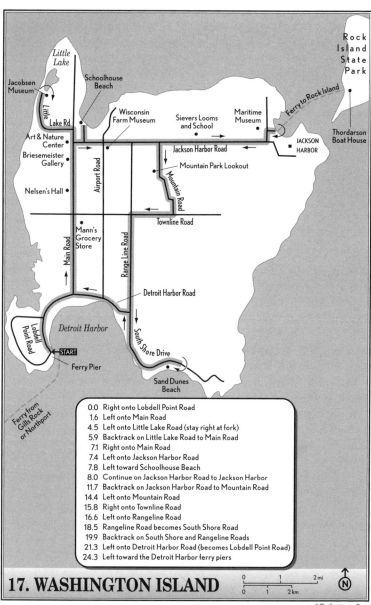

Little Lake

Rock Island State Park

Jacobsen Museum

Schoolhouse Beach

Little Lake Rd.

Wisconsin Farm Museum

Sievers Looms and School

Maritime Museum

Ferry to Rock Island

Art & Nature Center

Jackson Harbor Road

JACKSON HARBOR

Thordarson Boat House

Briesemeister Gallery

Airport Road

Mountain Park Lookout

Nelsen's Hall

Mountain Road

Townline Road

Mann's Grocery Store

Main Road

Range Line Road

Detroit Harbor Road

Lobdell Point Road

Detroit Harbor

South Shore Drive

START

Ferry Pier

Sand Dunes Beach

Ferry from Gills Rock or Northport

0.0	Right onto Lobdell Point Road
1.6	Left onto Main Road
4.5	Left onto Little Lake Road (stay right at fork)
5.9	Backtrack on Little Lake Road to Main Road
7.1	Right onto Main Road
7.4	Left onto Jackson Harbor Road
7.8	Left toward Schoolhouse Beach
8.0	Continue on Jackson Harbor Road to Jackson Harbor
11.7	Backtrack on Jackson Harbor Road to Mountain Road
14.4	Left onto Mountain Road
15.8	Right onto Townline Road
16.6	Left onto Rangeline Road
18.5	Rangeline Road becomes South Shore Road
19.9	Backtrack on South Shore and Rangeline Roads
21.3	Left onto Detroit Harbor Road (becomes Lobdell Point Road)
24.3	Left toward the Detroit Harbor ferry piers

17. WASHINGTON ISLAND

0   1   2 mi
0   1   2 km

N

© The Countryman Press

passage, through the infamous Death's Door strait, takes about 30 minutes. Don't worry—the recommended vessels have a good safety record.

There are several restaurants and a grocery store on the island. Lodging is available at the Dor-Cros Inn (920-847-2126), Findlay's Holiday Inn (920-847-2526), and Froghollow Farm Bed and Breakfast (920-847-2835) across from Sievers School of Fiber Arts. There are also many cottages for rent by the day or week.

To get to Gills Rock, take WI 42 North. To reach Northport, continue on WI 42 for about 2 miles beyond Gills Rock, where the road ends. This tour begins at Detroit Harbor on Washington Island, near the bike rental concession at the Island Clipper pier.

0.0 Right onto Lobdell Point Road.

1.6 Left onto Main Road through "downtown."
Mann's Grocery Store has a deli counter if you need to pick up lunch supplies. Mann's Mercantile in the Den Norske Grenda (Norwegian Village) complex offers souvenirs.

2.7 To your left is Nelsen's Hall, Bitter's Pub and Restaurant.
Bicyclists have waited out many a rain shower at this legendary bar that began as a bootlegging operation during Prohibition. The establishment gained a reputation for "treating" thirsty patrons with angostura bitters, which was considered to have medicinal value and, despite its high alcohol content, was not banned. Take the cure—a shot glass of bitters followed by a chaser of beer—and you will receive a Bitter's Club Membership Card for your wallet. Hot chocolate, soup, and sandwiches are also available.

3.6 To your left is the Briesemeister Gallery, which sells island-made paintings, pottery, and textiles.

4.3 To your left is the Art and Nature Center (920-847-2025).
This 90-year-old schoolhouse contains exhibits devoted to island history and rotating displays of artwork by island residents. If you're lucky, you may catch one of the artists performing a new composition on the piano or demonstrating watercolor painting.
Continue straight on Main Road.

4.5 Left onto Little Lake Road. Stay right at the fork.

Door County is a bicyclist's delight.

5.9 Jacobsen's Museum on Little Lake.
*This tiny cedar log cabin museum is chock-a-block full of natural and historic arti-
facts from the island. Every faded photograph tells a story, which the curators are
quick to relate if you show curiosity.*
    Backtrack on Little Lake Road to Main Road.

7.1 Right onto Main Road.

7.4 Left onto Jackson Harbor Road.

7.8 Left toward Schoolhouse Beach.
*The shore here is covered with smooth, rounded, white rocks, which are better for
stone skipping than beach sitting. Wait for Sand Dunes Beach, later in the ride, if
you plan on sunbathing.*
    Backtrack to Jackson Harbor Road and turn left.

10.1 Sievers Looms and School of Fiber Arts (920-847-2264) is to your left.
*Sievers Looms is the distributor of island-built birch and cherry weaving looms. A
small shop on the premises sells yarns spun from the wool of island sheep and items
made by students and teachers. The School of Fiber Arts offers weeklong and*

weekend classes on weaving, quilting, spinning, knitting, basketry, and papermaking during the summer months.

11.7 Continue on Jackson Harbor Road to Jackson Harbor.
Here the sprightly little Karfi ferry (920-493-6444) will take you to Rock Island State Park, a 10-minute trip. This 905-acre island was once the private estate of millionaire investor Chester Thordarson, whose castlelike boathouse is visible from Jackson Harbor. Now the island offers hiking, mountain biking (there are no paved roads), and primitive camping. Also at Jackson Harbor is a small maritime museum housed in converted fishing sheds. Methods of setting nets and processing fish for market are shown in photographs and exhibits.

Backtrack on Jackson Harbor Road to Mountain Road.

14.4 Left onto Mountain Road.

14.9 Tower Wayside.
Climb the observation tower for a sea gull's view of the island. Rest rooms and a picnic area are available.

Right from Wayside onto Mountain Road.

15.8 Right onto Townline Road.

16.6 Left onto Rangeline Road.

18.5 Continue past the marina. Rangeline Road becomes South Shore Road.

19.9 Sand Dunes Beach.
Take off your shoes and wiggle your toes in the sugar-fine sand at this scenic swimming beach. Remember to allow about 20 minutes to get back to the ferry pier from here.

Exit the beach area and backtrack on South Shore and Rangeline Roads.

21.3 Left onto Detroit Harbor Road, which becomes Lobdell Point Road.

24.3 Left toward the Detroit Harbor ferry piers.

Bicycle Repair Service

Nor Door Cyclery, 4007 WI 42, Fish Creek; 920-868-2275

NORTHERN
WISCONSIN

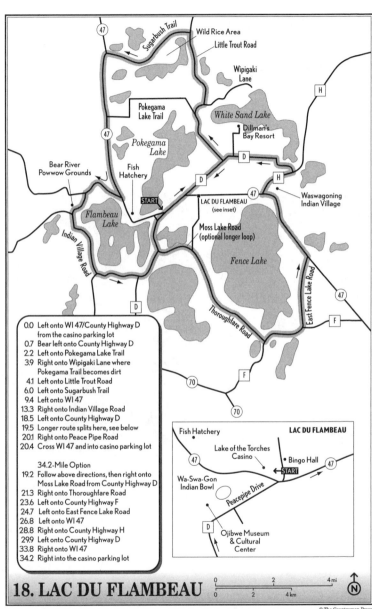

47 Sugarbush Trail   Wild Rice Area
                     Little Trout Road

                         Wipigaki
                         Lane

            Pokegama
            Lake Trail   White Sand Lake

47   Dillman's
        Pokegama   Bay Resort
        Lake
                            D
Bear River   Fish   D   H
Powwow Grounds Hatchery
                    START   47
                         LAC DU FLAMBEAU   Waswagoning
      Flambeau   (see inset)   Indian Village
      Lake
                    Moss Lake Road
Indian Village Road (optional longer loop)

                         Fence Lake
                                        East Fence Lake Road
                    D   47

                         Thoroughfare Road   F

0.0 Left onto WI 47/County Highway D   F
     from the casino parking lot
0.7 Bear left onto County Highway D   70
2.2 Left onto Pokegama Lake Trail
3.9 Right onto Wipigaki Lane where   70
     Pokegama Trail becomes dirt
4.1 Left onto Little Trout Road
6.0 Left onto Sugarbush Trail   Fish Hatchery   LAC DU FLAMBEAU
9.4 Left onto WI 47
13.3 Right onto Indian Village Road   47   Lake of the Torches
18.5 Left onto County Highway D   Casino   • Bingo Hall
19.5 Longer route splits here, see below   START   47
20.1 Right onto Peace Pipe Road   Wa-Swa-Gon
20.4 Cross WI 47 and into casino parking lot Indian Bowl
                                                    Peacepipe Drive
     34.2-Mile Option
19.2 Follow above directions, then right onto   D
     Moss Lake Road from County Highway D   Ojibwe Museum
21.3 Right onto Thoroughfare Road   & Cultural
23.6 Left onto County Highway F   Center
24.7 Left onto East Fence Lake Road
26.8 Left onto WI 47
28.8 Right onto County Highway H
29.9 Left onto County Highway D
33.8 Right onto WI 47
34.2 Right into the casino parking lot

18. LAC DU FLAMBEAU

0   2   4 mi
0   2   4 km

N

© The Countryman Press

Lac du Flambeau

- **DISTANCE:** 20.4 or 34.2 miles
- **TERRAIN:** Flat to gently rolling

Deerskin moccasins bounce to the beat of ceremonial drums each week when powwows are held on the reservation of the Lac du Flambeau band of the Lake Superior Chippewa. This entire tour takes place within reservation boundaries and offers rare opportunities to glimpse a bald eagle circling over the site of a fierce Indian battle or to see a canoe slipping silently through a marsh during the wild rice harvest.

The route skirts the shores of the 10-lake Lac du Flambeau chain. The terrain is almost perfectly flat and the road paved, though subject to frequent frost heaves. The route is heavily forested with pines and birches.

The Chippewa are an Algonquin-language eastern tribe, originally called Ojibwe, a word that translates as "to roast until puckered up," referring to the characteristically puckered seams of their moccasins. The word *Ojibwe* was mispronounced by white traders and became Chippewa. The Chippewa referred to themselves as "the writing people" because of their habit of drawing on birch bark. The Lac du Flambeau people have grown from a small band to a tribe of just over two thousand members, governed by a tribal council of twelve.

Fur traders named the lake that dominates the area, Lac du Flambeau, French for "lake of the torches," when they observed

the Chippewa spearfishing at night by the light of flaming torches. Recent years have seen a renewed interest in spearfishing and
other Chippewa customs. Like other Wisconsin tribes, the Chippewa have benefited from rulings permitting reservation gaming
and have recently opened a casino and bingo hall.

To reach Lac du Flambeau, take WI 47 to County Highway D.
You may park at the Lake of the Torches Casino (1-800-258-6724),
which is located at the corner of WI 47 and Peace Pipe Drive. The
casino is open 24 hours every day and offers blackjack, slot
machines, and video poker. There is also lodging and food available.

If you follow Peace Pipe Drive into the village, you may visit
the Lac du Flambeau Museum and Cultural Center (715-588-
3333), a well-organized facility that includes an authentic 24-foot
dugout canoe, examples of Native American clothing, and an
exhibit depicting Chippewa activities during various times of the
year. There is also a gift shop that sells traditional Native American crafts. Hours are Monday through Saturday, 10 AM to 4 PM.
Adjacent to the museum is the Wa-Swa-Gon Indian Bowl (call the
cultural center for information), where powwows are held on
Tuesday evenings at 7 PM, mid-June through mid-August. The
Indian Bowl also contains a replica of a Native American village
with wigwams, hide and fish racks, and wild rice finishing areas.
The mileage for this tour starts at the main entrance/exit of the
casino.

0.0 Left onto WI 47/County Highway D from the casino parking lot.

0.7 Bear left onto County Highway D.

2.2 Left onto Pokegama Lake Trail.

3.9 Right onto Wipigaki Lane where Pokegama Trail becomes dirt.

4.1 Left onto Little Trout Road.
*Wild rice is harvested from the marshes along this stretch beginning in mid-
August. Tribal members ply the waterways in pairs of canoes. When the rice plants
are located, the 4- to 8-foot stalks are bent over one canoe and beaten with a stick
to loosen the kernels, which fall to the bottom of the boat. The stalks are then beat-
en in the opposite direction over the other canoe. Sacks of the purplish-black deli-*

Morning mist hangs over Indian Village Road.

cacy (some of which is now planted, not really wild) are available for sale in local shops.

6.0 Left onto Sugarbush Trail at the bottom of the hill. This turn is easy to miss.

9.4 Left onto WI 47 (a busy road but with a good shoulder).

13.3 Right onto Indian Village Road.

15.2 The parallel road to your left leads to the site of an old Indian village; nothing remains today.
The Chippewa lived a nomadic existence, traveling between the shores of Lake Superior, where they fished in the summer, and Lac du Flambeau, where they fished, tapped trees for maple sugar, hunted, and harvested wild rice during other seasons. They used birch bark to construct their homes, called wigwams, and their canoes. A small group led by Chief Sharpened Stone arrived here in 1745 and found the area so appealing they decided to settle permanently. Their presence was challenged by the Sioux, culminating in a fierce battle on the lake's Strawberry Island (visible at various points of this ride) where the Chippewa emerged as the victors.

The French claimed sovereignty of the area during a ceremony held at Sault St. Marie in 1671. The fur trade peaked in 1815 when John Jacob Astor's American Fur Company dominated area commerce. An 1853 treaty established the Chippewa on reservations, including the one at Lac du Flambeau. The greatest upheaval in Flambeau history was probably the opening of the reservation to logging in the 1880s. The industry thrived to the benefit of timber barons and the detriment of the forest, which was severely overcut. Visitors to the Flambeau Lumber Company were housed at a local hotel and were the first to broadcast the area's fishing and vacation appeal.

To your right, looking across the Bear River to the peninsula, are the Bear River Powwow grounds, where large intertribal gatherings are held. The Bear River was an important water route, linking Lac du Flambeau with the Wisconsin River and eventually Lake Superior.

18.5 Left onto County Highway D.

19.2 Moss Lake Road. If you are taking the 34.2-mile option, turn right here and skip to directions below.

20.1 Right onto Peace Pipe Drive. Follow through downtown Lac du Flambeau.

20.4 Cross WI 47 and into the Lake of the Torches Casino parking lot.

34.2-MILE OPTION

19.2 Follow above directions, then take a right onto Moss Lake Road from County Highway D.

20.6 Mink farm.

21.3 Right onto Thoroughfare Road.

23.6 Left onto County Highway F.

24.7 Left onto East Fence Lake Road.
On this road is the Lighthouse Resort, purchased in 1950 by the Johnson Wax Company of Racine, Wisconsin, as a vacation retreat for its employees.

26.8 Left onto WI 47.

28.8 Right onto County Highway H.

29.1 Waswagoning re-created Ojibwe village (715-588-2615).
Walk back in time to when the Ojibwe built wigwams and moved from area to area as the seasons changed. Hands-on viewing of wigwams, willow fish traps, birch-bark baskets, bows and arrows, spears, and hides. You may also try your hand at some native games and crafts. Hours are Tuesday through Saturday, 10 AM to 4 PM, mid-May through the end of September.

29.9 Left onto County Highway D.

31.9 Though the route continues straight, a right turn here will take you to Dillman's Bay Resort (715-588-3143).
This is a top-notch resort with a stunning location on a 1,200-acre peninsula jutting out into White Sand Lake. Established in 1934, this was one of the first resorts in the area, and it continues to be run by the founding family. The resort has carved out a unique niche by offering artists' workshops led by well-known painters.

33.8 Right onto WI 47.

34.2 Right into the casino parking lot.
A worthwhile side trip is a visit to the Tribal Council Fish Hatchery (715-588-3307) at the lower end of Pokegama Lake on WI 47. More than 40 million trout, walleye, and muskellunge eggs are hatched annually, raised to fingerling sizes, and planted in local lakes. The facility also has a catch-and-keep trout-fishing pond.

Bicycle Repair Service

BJ's Sport Shop, 917 WI 51 North, Minocqua; 715-356-3900

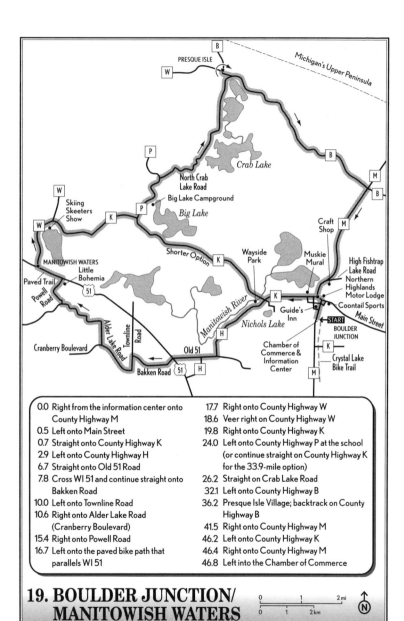

0.0 Right from the information center onto County Highway M	17.7 Right onto County Highway W
0.5 Left onto Main Street	18.6 Veer right on County Highway W
0.7 Straight onto County Highway K	19.8 Right onto County Highway K
2.9 Left onto County Highway H	24.0 Left onto County Highway P at the school (or continue straight on County Highway K for the 33.9-mile option)
6.7 Straight onto Old 51 Road	
7.8 Cross WI 51 and continue straight onto Bakken Road	26.2 Straight on Crab Lake Road
	32.1 Left onto County Highway B
10.0 Left onto Townline Road	36.2 Presque Isle Village; backtrack on County Highway B
10.6 Right onto Alder Lake Road (Cranberry Boulevard)	
	41.5 Right onto County Highway M
15.4 Right onto Powell Road	46.2 Left onto County Highway K
16.7 Left onto the paved bike path that parallels WI 51	46.4 Right onto County Highway M
	46.8 Left into the Chamber of Commerce

19. BOULDER JUNCTION/ MANITOWISH WATERS

0   1   2 mi
0   1   2 km

N

© The Countryman Press

Boulder Junction/ Manitowish Waters

- **DISTANCE**: 33.9 or 46.8 miles
- **TERRAIN**: Gently rolling to rolling

Flannel shirts are *haute couture* in this area, which most Mid-westerners simply refer to as "up north." For many, just breathing the pine-scented air brings back childhood memories of summers spent at the family cabin, fishing with a cane pole or floating idly in an inner tube.

Wisconsin writer Robert Gard summed up the feeling this area evokes. "Something happens to me when I go up to northern Wisconsin," he wrote. "Perhaps it's because the sky and woods and lakes still have an edge of wildness... you can definitely experience a feeling that you are alone, and for a moment, you have intimate knowledge of the secret of solitude."

Manitowish Waters and Presque Isle are small towns with a few shops selling such unlikely combinations as baked goods, bait, and souvenirs. Boulder Junction is slightly larger and has several lodging options, including the Northern Highlands Motor Lodge (715-385-2150), which has a living room with fireplace, a swimming pool, and a Jacuzzi. Owner Jim Galloway can suggest other road bike or mountain bike trips. Satisfy your post-ride appetite with dinner at the Guide's Inn (715-385-2233), where chef Jimmy Dean VanRosson prepares walleyed pike and other North Country specialties with a flair. Call ahead for reservations. The Outdoorsman Restaurant (715-385-2826) in downtown Boulder Junction serves hearty breakfasts and has a great selection of fresh fruit pies.

The tour begins at the Boulder Junction Chamber of Commerce and Information Center, located on County Highway M just south of the center of town. To get there, take WI 51 to County Highway M. Follow County Highway M north to Boulder Junction. The information center is adjacent to a park with rest rooms and a picnic area.

This tour follows some of the scenic back roads in the area, but the information center is also the starting point for the new Boulder Junction Bike Trail System. This is a 13.5-mile paved trail that extends south past Trout Lake, through the Northern Highlands State Forest, and to the Crystal Lake Campground. You can get a trail map at the information center.

0.0 Right from the information center onto County Highway M.

0.5 Left onto Main Street.

0.7 Straight on County Highway K where County Highway M goes right.

1.1 On the water tank to your right is a mural depicting the town mascot, the muskie—short for muskellunge, Wisconsin's top trophy fish.
Boulder Junction has dubbed itself "the muskie capital of the world," a title it holds with the official endorsement of the United States Trademark Office.

The Native American word for this predaceous member of the pike family is masquinong. *Muskies commonly reach a weight of 70 pounds and a length exceeding 4 feet. The head has long, thin, powerful jaws that house a set of needle-sharp teeth. Owing to its position at the top of the food chain and its reputation as a moody loner, hundreds of legends have evolved around the annual "muskie hunt." The heaviest concentration of muskie lakes is in the headwaters region of the Chippewa, Flambeau, and Wisconsin Rivers.*

2.9 Left onto County Highway H.
The wayside park on the right borders the Manitowish River. A canoe trip down this wild and scenic river is a wonderful afternoon voyage. Eagle sightings are almost guaranteed. Call Schauss Woodworking (715-385-2434) for canoe rental and transport. On the opposite side of the road, a 1-mile detour will take you to the Nichols Lake picnic area, which has rest rooms.

6.7 Straight onto Old 51 Road where County Highway H goes left.

7.8 Cross US 51 and continue straight onto Bakken Road.

10.0 Left onto Townline Road.

10.6 Right onto Alder Lake Road (Cranberry Boulevard).
Six cranberry growers are represented on this stretch of road. The cranberry harvest takes place in late September when the bogs are artificially flooded, causing berry-laden vines to float to the surface. Several methods of "wet picking" are used.

One method employs a machine, which is either pushed or ridden by the operator, that uses teeth to lift berries from the vine. This is a variation on the hand rake, a boxlike apparatus commonly used to scoop up berries from the bog before the process was mechanized. Hand rakes are still used for hard-to-reach places. The berries are deposited into plastic boats, which are towed by tractors to a loading area.

Another method, called the water reel, lifts berries off the vine to float on top of the flooded bed. They are then corralled to a corner and loaded into trucks by elevators. Growers are paid according to the quantity, quality, and color of berries they deliver to the processing plants.

15.4 Right onto Powell Road.

16.7 Left onto the paved bike path that parallels US 51.
To the right about 1 mile is Little Bohemia Restaurant and Lodge (715-543-8433), a resort on Little Star Lake where notorious underworld character John Dillinger escaped under the noses of FBI agents in 1934. Dillinger, Baby Face Nelson, and several other gangsters had rented rooms at the hotel. Federal agents got a tip that Dillinger was in the area and were hot on his trail. When they fired on a suspicious car, killing one innocent local and wounding two more, Dillinger, who was inside the lodge, heard the shots and fled. In his haste, he left behind a toothbrush and a box of laxatives, which are on display, along with other memorabilia, in the restaurant's Dillinger Room.

17.7 Right onto County Highway W. This is a busy road, but it has a paved bike lane.

18.2 The town of Manitowish Waters consists mainly of lakefront vacation properties.
The village center is small, with several restaurants and a grocery store. Manitowish *is a Native American word meaning "evil spirit."*

18.3 The Frank B. Koller Memorial Park is "downtown," next to the bait shop with the giant fiberglass bass outside. Continue on County Highway W on the outskirts of town.

18.6 Veer right on County Highway W.

19.0 The Skiing Skeeters, a local water-ski club, performs here during the summer months.
Visitors to Wisconsin's North Woods will be impressed with the professional caliber of small-town ski shows. Many of these talented youngsters, who begin skiing as tots, go on to win national competitions or ski at Florida's Cypress Gardens. There is usually no admission charge—a hat is passed to cover club expenses. Check with local chambers of commerce for show schedules.

19.8 Right onto County Highway K.

24.0 Left onto County Highway P at the school.
Alternate route: *For the 33.9-mile option, continue straight here on County Highway K and follow it back into the village of Boulder Junction.*

25.2 Big Lake Campground is to your right.
There are rest rooms and a nice swimming beach. It is about 1½ miles in and out.

26.2 Straight on Crab Lake Road where County Highway P goes left.
Crab Lake Road ranks among our favorite cycling roads in Wisconsin. Just as you've fallen into a rhythmic, effortless cadence on this flat to barely rolling route, here it is—another of Wisconsin's geographic anomalies. The bold ridge and kettle topography along this road follow the spine of a terminal moraine more typical of the scenery in southern Wisconsin. In addition to its pleasing contours, the road is shaded by enormous hardwoods, which eluded the chain saw when the lumberjacks quested for timber. High points along the ridge overlook Crab Lake, which has several picturesque islands. This hilly pocket of the North Woods, combined with fertile plains for grain growing nearby, attracted a group of Kentuckians who ran an extensive moonshine operation here during Prohibition.

32.1 Left onto County Highway B.

36.2 Presque Isle, French for "nearly an island," has a park, grocery store, and restaurant. At this point you are about 1 mile south of the border with Michigan's Upper Peninsula.
In keeping with the fish theme, Presque Isle calls itself the "walleye capital of the

world." Don't be deceived when you pick up the Walleye Street Journal*—you won't find NYSE listings in Presque Isle's newsy little weekly.*
    Backtrack on County Highway B from downtown Presque Isle.

41.5 Right onto County Highway M.

45.4 To your left on High Fishtrap Lake Road is The Homestead.
This shop features local crafts to decorate your vacation home, ranging from a life-sized wooden Indian to a loon-shaped napkin holder.

46.2 Left onto County Highway K into downtown Boulder Junction.

46.4 Right onto County Highway M.

46.8 Left into the chamber of commerce.

Bicycle Repair Service

Coontail Sports, 5466 Park Street, Boulder Junction; 715-385-0250

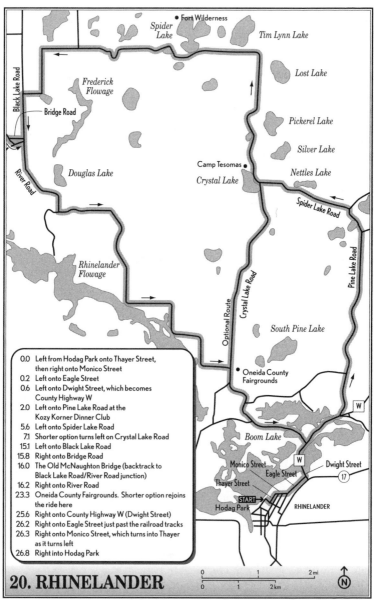

Spider Lake

Fort Wilderness

Tim Lynn Lake

Lost Lake

Black Lake Road

Frederick Flowage

Bridge Road

Pickerel Lake

Silver Lake

River Road

Douglas Lake

Camp Tesomas

Crystal Lake

Nettles Lake

Spider Lake Road

Rhinelander Flowage

Crystal Lake Road

Optional Route

Pine Lake Road

South Pine Lake

Oneida County Fairgrounds

0.0 Left from Hodag Park onto Thayer Street, then right onto Monico Street
0.2 Left onto Eagle Street
0.6 Left onto Dwight Street, which becomes County Highway W
2.0 Left onto Pine Lake Road at the Kozy Korner Dinner Club
5.6 Left onto Spider Lake Road
7.1 Shorter option turns left on Crystal Lake Road
15.1 Left onto Black Lake Road
15.8 Right onto Bridge Road
16.0 The Old McNaughton Bridge (backtrack to Black Lake Road/River Road junction)
16.2 Right onto River Road
23.3 Oneida County Fairgrounds. Shorter option rejoins the ride here
25.6 Right onto County Highway W (Dwight Street)
26.2 Right onto Eagle Street just past the railroad tracks
26.3 Right onto Monico Street, which turns into Thayer as it turns left
26.8 Right into Hodag Park

Boom Lake

W

W

Monico Street

Eagle Street

Dwight Street

Thayer Street

17

START

Hodag Park

RHINELANDER

0   1   2 mi
0   1   2 km

20. RHINELANDER

N

Rhinelander

- **DISTANCE:** 14 or 26.8 miles
- **TERRAIN:** Flat to gently rolling

On this pleasant spin through the deep North Woods, you are almost guaranteed to spot a white-tailed deer, raccoon, or porcupine. If you are lucky, you'll catch a glimpse of a bald eagle soaring over the Wisconsin River or a black bear feasting on roadside berries. But only those with keen senses and a vivid imagination will spot the elusive Hodag. In the late 1800s, lumberman Gene Shepherd showed pictures of a horrifying green and white creature with spines, horns, and sharp incisor teeth to fellow lumberjacks in the Rhinelander area. He reportedly used a chloroform-soaked sponge to capture the dinosaur-like Hodag while it was asleep in a cave. Shepherd kept curious visitors at bay, warning that the creature thrived on a steady diet of loggers and white bulldogs.

Rhinelander has kept this lumberjack legend alive by embracing the Hodag as its mascot. You can see a likeness of this beast on a statue in Pioneer Park, the water tower, and the sports jerseys of local high school teams.

The village of Rhinelander, settled in 1880, was a supply headquarters for logging teams who worked in northern Wisconsin and the Upper Peninsula of Michigan. The logging museum in Pioneer Park chronicles the era with photos, logging implements, and "ole Five Spot," a 1925 Baldwin 2-8-0 locomotive that was used by the

A flat, shady ride through Wisconsin's North Woods

Thunder Lake Railroad. You might also want to visit the historic Oneida County Courthouse, a turn-of-the-20th-century building with an outstanding collection of murals depicting life in pioneer days. The courthouse exterior is impressive at night when the dome's Tiffany glass windows are backlit. The beginning of this tour traverses forested land owned by logging companies. Later in the ride, the route follows the course of the Wisconsin River, used in the early days to transport logs. Today, the timber is delivered by truck; take care when being passed by logging vehicles—their size and speed create a draft that can be dangerous for cyclists.

Appropriately, the tour begins in Rhinelander's Hodag Park, which has a picnic shelter, rest rooms, and a beach on Bangs Lake. To get to the park, enter town on WI 17 from the north or south. Then follow Monico and Thayer Streets west to the park. The mileage begins at the park entrance/exit.

0.0 Left from Hodag Park onto Thayer Street for only about 100 yards. Right onto Monico Street.

0.2 Left onto Eagle Street.

0.6 Left onto Dwight Street. Follow Dwight Street out of town, where it becomes County Highway W.

2.0 Left onto Pine Lake Road at the Kozy Korner Dinner Club.

5.6 Left onto Spider Lake Road.

7.1 Junction with Crystal Lake Road, just before Camp Tesomas Boy Scout Camp.
This is the turnoff for the 14-mile ride. For the shorter option, turn left onto Crystal Lake Road and rejoin the longer route at the 23.3 mile mark below. The 26.8-mile route continues on Spider Lake Road.

8.7 The fields you are passing are owned by Frito-Lay.
You'll often see white-tailed deer feeding on the corn and wheat.

10.2 Tasmania Outback Stage and Grill.

13.1 Continue straight on Spider Lake Road at the Muskellunge Lake Road junction.

15.1 Left onto Black Lake Road.

15.8 Right onto Bridge Road.

16.0 The Old McNaughton Bridge.
On a warm summer day, you'll spot many canoeists paddling down the Wisconsin River at this point. It is also a good spot to take a dip and cool off before continuing the ride.
    Backtrack to the Black Lake Road/River Road junction.

16.2 Right onto River Road.

23.3 Oneida County Fairgrounds and home of the Hodag Country Music Fest.
This early July event is a sort of country Woodstock. The festival features performers such as the Oak Ridge Boys, Ronnie Milsap, and Kenny Rogers. This is where the shorter option rejoins the longer ride.

25.6 Right onto County Highway W (Dwight Street) where River Road ends.

26.2 Right onto Eagle Street just past the railroad tracks.

26.3 Right onto Monico Street, which turns into Thayer as it turns left.

26.8 Right into Hodag Park.

Bicycle Repair Service

Bikes and Boards, 1670 North Stevens, Rhinelander; 715-369-1999

21

Chequamegon National Forest

- **DISTANCE:** 24.5 or 38.7 miles
- **TERRAIN:** Rolling to hilly

This tour traverses the Chequamegon National Forest, an 844,000-acre parcel of public land larger than the state of Rhode Island. Chequamegon, a tongue twister used by Wisconsin Public Radio as a test for apprentice announcers, comes from the Chippewa language. The accepted pronunciation is "Sho-wa-me-gon," with the accent on the second syllable. Translations vary from "long strip of land" to "soft beaver dam."

The population of Cable, starting point of the tour, swells from its normal 800 residents to as many as 20,000 during two world-class sporting events held annually: the American Birkebeiner cross-country ski marathon in February and the Chequamegon Fat-Tire Festival in September. The Birkebeiner follows a 55-kilometer course through the forest between Telemark Lodge in Cable and the town of Hayward. A 27-kilometer course called the Kortelopet is also offered. The event is patterned after the Birkebeiner held each year in Lillehammer, Norway, which celebrates the rescue of a Norwegian prince from enemy soldiers in 1206. The word *birkebeiner,* which means "birch legs," refers to the primitive handcrafted skis worn by early Norsemen.

Telemark Lodge also hosts the Chequamegon Fat-Tire Festival, which has made a name for the area as the Midwest's mountain biking mecca. Mountain bike enthusiasts can pick up a comprehensive trail map from the Chamber of Commerce or write to

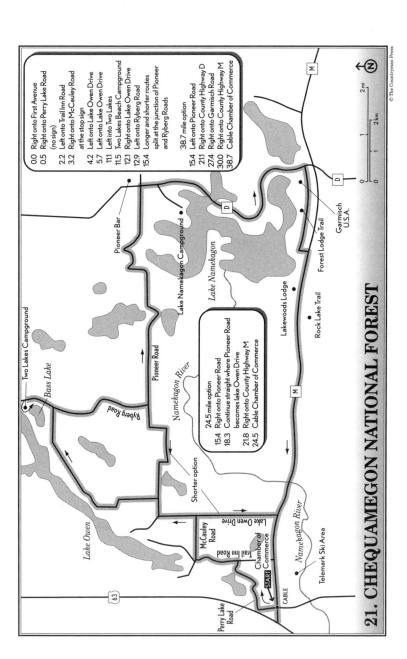

21. CHEQUAMEGON NATIONAL FOREST

0.0	Right onto First Avenue
0.5	Right onto Perry Lake Road
2.2	Left onto Trail Inn Road (no sign)
3.2	Right onto McCauley Road at the stop sign
4.2	Left onto Lake Owen Drive
5.7	Left onto Lake Owen Drive
11.1	Left into Two Lakes
11.5	Two Lakes Beach Campground
12.1	Right onto Lake Owen Drive
12.9	Left onto Ryberg Road
15.4	Longer and shorter routes split at the junction of Pioneer and Ryberg Roads

38.7 mile option

15.4	Left onto Pioneer Road
21.1	Right onto County Highway D
27.4	Right onto Garmisch Road
30.0	Right onto County Highway M
38.7	Cable Chamber of Commerce

24.5 mile option

15.4	Right onto Pioneer Road
18.3	Continue straight where Pioneer Road becomes Lake Owen Drive
21.8	Right onto County Highway M
24.5	Cable Chamber of Commerce

Two Lakes Campground

Bass Lake

Lake Owen

Pioneer Bar

Ryberg Road

Pioneer Road

Lake Namekagon Campground

Lake Namekagon

Namekagon River

Shorter option

Lakewoods Lodge

Rock Lake Trail

Forest Lodge Trail

Garmisch U.S.A.

McCauley Road

Trail Inn Road

Lake Owen Drive

Chamber of Commerce

START

CABLE

Perry Lake Road

Namekagon River

Telemark Ski Area

63

© The Countryman Press

Chequamegon Area Mountain Bike Association (CAMBA) at P.O. Box 141, Cable, WI 54821 (1-800-533-7454). This organization has produced a map that shows the location of trailheads in the Chequamegon region. If you're looking for an off-road diversion, mountain bikes may be rented from New Moon Mountain Biking in Hayward (715-634-8685), Riverbrook Bike and Ski in Seeley (715-634-5600), and at Telemark Lodge (715-798-3999).

This tour begins at the Cable Area Chamber of Commerce on WI 63 and County Highway M in downtown Cable.

0.0 Right onto First Avenue, and ride north past the Bon Nuit Motel.

0.5 Right onto Perry Lake Road (no sign) at the intersection where First Avenue ends.

1.4 Perry Lake Road makes a sharp turn to the left. The boat landing and beach are ahead.

2.2 Left onto Trail Inn Road where Perry Lake Road ends.

3.2 Right onto McCauley Road at the stop sign, where Resort Road goes left and Trail Inn Road goes straight.

4.2 Left onto Lake Owen Drive where McCauley Road ends.

5.7 Left onto Lake Owen Drive toward Eagle Knob, where Pioneer Road goes straight.

11.1 Left into Two Lakes Campground (715-739-6334).
Located between Lake Owen and Bass Lake, this is one of many beautiful campgrounds in the Chequamegon National Forest. All have primitive facilities, with water pumps and pit toilets. For those who prefer pure wilderness, camping is allowed anywhere in the national forest, as long as you are at least 50 feet from a lake or stream.

11.5 The Two Lakes Campground Beach.
Rest rooms and water are available at the beach. Follow the left fork just after you leave the beach. Continue between the lakes and back to Lake Owen Drive.

12.1 Right onto Lake Owen Drive.

12.9 Left onto Ryberg Road.

Spinning through Chequamegon National Forest

15.4 At the junction of Pioneer and Ryberg Roads, the longer and shorter routes split.
The following directions are for the 38.7-mile option. If you are riding the 24.5-mile option, skip ahead to the shorter route directions.

38.7-MILE OPTION

15.4 Left onto Pioneer Road where Ryberg Road ends.

21.1 Right onto County Highway D at the Pioneer Bar.

21.7 Lake Namekagon Campground and Picnic Area. Picnic tables and rest rooms are available here.

27.4 Right onto Garmisch Road just before reaching County Highway M.

28.4 This is the road to Garmisch U.S.A.
This old world–style Bavarian lodge dates to the 1920s, when it was a private vaca-

tion retreat for a wealthy Chicago family. It's worth a peek into the great room of the main lodge, where the décor centers around an unusual stuffed menagerie.

29.1 Forest Lodge Nature Trail.
This self-guided trail, operated by the Cable Natural History Museum, gives a good introduction to North Country fauna with a walk through a restored prairie, bog, and hemlock forest.

30.0 Right onto County Highway M.

30.8 The Rock Lake Trail is a favorite with mountain bikers, hikers, and cross-country skiers.
Rest rooms are available here.

36.4 Telemark Resort turnoff.
Telemark has a world-class network of cross-country ski trails where international competitions such as the American Birkebeiner are held each year. There is also downhill skiing. The cross-country ski trails are open to mountain bikers during the warmer months. It is about a 2-mile detour to ride through the resort.

38.7 You're back in the village of Cable.

24.5-MILE OPTION

15.4 Right onto Pioneer Road, where the 38.7-mile route turns left.

18.3 Continue straight where Pioneer Road becomes South Lake Owen Drive.

21.8 Right onto County Highway M. This is a busy road, but it has an ample shoulder.

22.2 Telemark Resort turnoff (see above).

24.5 You're back in Cable at the Chamber of Commerce.

Bicycle Repair Service

New Moon Bike Shop, 15569 North US Highway 63, Hayward; 715-634-8685
Riverbrook Bike and Ski, 13493 North US Highway 63, Seeley; 715-634-5600

BAYFIELD
PENINSULA

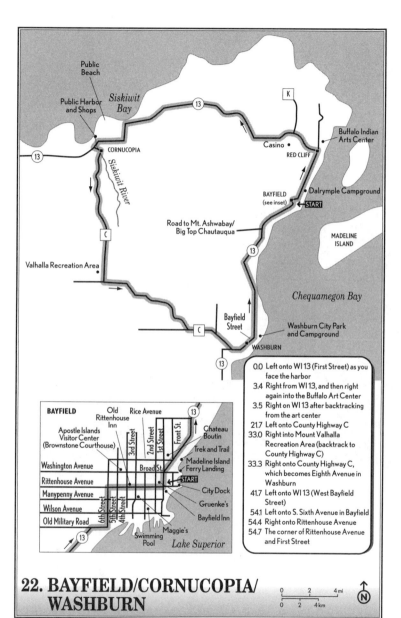

Public Beach

Siskiwit Bay

Public Harbor and Shops

13

K

13

Buffalo Indian Arts Center

Casino

CORNUCOPIA

RED CLIFF

13

Siskiwit River

BAYFIELD (see inset)

Dalrymple Campground

START

C

Road to Mt. Ashwabay/ Big Top Chautauqua

MADELINE ISLAND

13

Valhalla Recreation Area

Chequamegon Bay

Bayfield Street

C

Washburn City Park and Campground

WASHBURN

13

0.0 Left onto WI 13 (First Street) as you face the harbor

3.4 Right from WI 13, and then right again into the Buffalo Art Center

3.5 Right on WI 13 after backtracking from the art center

21.7 Left onto County Highway C

33.0 Right into Mount Valhalla Recreation Area (backtrack to County Highway C)

33.3 Right onto County Highway C, which becomes Eighth Avenue in Washburn

41.7 Left onto WI 13 (West Bayfield Street)

54.1 Left onto S. Sixth Avenue in Bayfield

54.4 Right onto Rittenhouse Avenue

54.7 The corner of Rittenhouse Avenue and First Street

BAYFIELD

Old Rittenhouse Inn

Rice Avenue

13

Apostle Islands Visitor Center (Brownstone Courthouse)

3rd Street

2nd Street

1st Street

Front St.

Chateau Boutin

Trek and Trail

Washington Avenue

Broad St.

Madeline Island Ferry Landing

Rittenhouse Avenue

START

Manypenny Avenue

City Dock

Wilson Avenue

6th Street

5th Street

4th Street

Gruenke's

Old Military Road

Bayfield Inn

13

Swimming Pool

Maggie's

Lake Superior

22. BAYFIELD/CORNUCOPIA/ WASHBURN

0   2   4 mi

0   2   4 km

N

Bayfield/Cornucopia/Washburn

- **DISTANCE:** 54.7 miles
- **TERRAIN:** Rolling

After a century of boom and bust economies based on fur trading, lumbering, commercial fishing, and brownstone quarrying, Bayfield has finally settled comfortably and profitably into the tourism niche. Today's visitor is content to reap only the spectacular views of Lake Superior and the glittering offshore archipelago known as the Apostle Islands.

Biking in the Bayfield area is best combined with some offshore exploration aboard one of several vessels. The Apostle Islands Cruise Service (715-779-3925) offers several sight-seeing voyages that depart daily from the Bayfield dock. These cruises are extremely popular—advance booking is suggested. Sailing charters and sea kayak trips can be arranged through Trek and Trail (715-779-3595) on Washington Avenue or Sailboats, Inc. (715-779-3269) on Front Street.

Relentless lobbying by Wisconsin senator Gaylord Nelson led to the creation of the Apostle Islands National Lakeshore by the United States Senate in 1969. All of the islands except the most developed, Madeline Island, are included in this designation. How the Apostles got their name is always fodder for a feud, since no matter how you count, there are more than a dozen of them. While several transitory sand spits are sometimes included and sometimes not, the generally accepted total is 22, including Madeline Island.

Some say the label originated with a French explorer and priest who followed tradition by granting the islands a name with religious significance. Others say the name came from a gang of thieves known as the Apostles who used the islands as their base. In 1820, scientist and explorer Henry Schoolcraft suggested calling the chain the Federation Islands and giving each island the name of a state—his proposal garnered little support.

A walking-tour map titled "Bargeboard and Brownstone," available from local businesses, guides the visitor past Bayfield's most impressive buildings. Turn-of-the-20th-century timber barons favored the eye-catching Queen Anne style, characterized by a variety of surface textures, multiple gables, turrets, and sweeping porches that allowed them to savor the view and the cool lake breezes. People of more modest means built rectangular, one-and-a-half story houses with steep roofs to shed heavy snows in the winter. These homes were traditionally made of wood logged from local forests and painted white.

The former Bayfield County Courthouse, located on Washington Avenue between Fourth and Fifth Streets, is a stunning example of local brownstone construction. The building has served as a school, World War II German prisoner-of-war camp, and currently as the Apostle Islands Lakeshore Visitor Center.

The town was named after Lieutenant Henry Bayfield of the British Navy, who made the first accurate navigational charts of the Apostle Islands and Chequamegon Bay. Lieutenant Bayfield joined forces with Minnesota legislator Henry Rice to establish the town in hopes of it becoming a major Great Lakes port to compete with Duluth and Chicago.

Follow WI 13 North to Bayfield. The tour begins at the junction of First Street and Rittenhouse Avenue, in front of the Bayfield Inn. Behind the inn is a gazebo known as the Waiting Pavilion. Built in 1913 by the Bayfield Civic League at a cost of $300, it is still used as a speaker's platform, band shell, and shelter for boat passengers.

0.0 Left onto WI 13 (First Street) as you face the harbor.
As you climb the hill out of town, enjoy a spectacular view of the lake to your right.

There's little doubt why lumber baron Frank Boutin Jr. chose this site for the splendid yellow house that stands on the hillside above you. Called Chateau Boutin, the building is now a bed-and-breakfast inn, operated in conjunction with the Old Rittenhouse Inn. The home's combination of sandstone, brick, and clapboard construction is characteristic of the Queen Anne style.

0.6 Dalrymple Park Campground (715-779-5712) is to your right.
This 30-site facility with a prime location on the Lake Superior shore is operated by the city of Bayfield. The campground is named for entrepreneur William Dalrymple, who in 1883 began construction on a railroad to connect the port of Bayfield with his huge wheat farms in Minnesota and North Dakota. Only 4 miles of track were laid before Dalrymple's death, and an economic crisis put an end to the grand scheme.

2.7 You are now entering the reservation of the Red Cliff band of the Lake Superior Chippewa.
The Chippewa arrived here in the 1500s, escaping the threat of the Iroquois who dominated the area to the east. They found the Superior area populated by the Dakota nation, whom they easily suppressed. When the French arrived, the Chippewa established a friendly and beneficial trading relationship that lasted more than a century. Pressure to open up northern Wisconsin to logging and settlement led to the Treaty of 1854 when the reservation was formed. About 600 Chippewa tribe members now live on the 7,000-acre reservation.

3.4 Right from WI 13, and then right again into the Buffalo Art Center.
The center offers contemporary art displays, artifacts, and a gift shop selling Native American–made items. Across the road is the newly built Isle Vista Casino, which offers blackjack and slot machine gaming. A bingo hall is adjacent to the casino.

3.5 Right on WI 13 after backtracking from the art center.

5.8 The Buffalo Store is your last chance to buy provisions for the next 15 miles.

20.2 Known locally as "Cornie," Cornucopia is Wisconsin's northernmost community.
This old fishing village is located on Siskiwit Bay, where the Siskiwit River flows into Lake Superior. The Chippewa called the bay Siskawekaning, which means "where the fish can be caught." Polish and Czechoslovakian immigrants who worked in the

lumber industry built the impressive Russian Orthodox church with its octagonal tower that still stands on Erie Avenue.

21.1 Right onto Siskiwit Bay Parkway, which leads to the Cornucopia Wayside Park.
Here you will find water, rest rooms, and a picnic shelter. Follow the driveway to Cornucopia Public Harbor shops.

21.3 The Good Earth Shop, Blue Raven Antiques, and Hart Handweaving are all worth a visit.
The Good Earth sells books, cards, juices, and healthy snacks. Take a breather at an outdoor table overlooking the Cornucopia marina, where stubby white Great Lakes fishing boats brush elbows with snazzy sailboats.
    Continue on WI 13 for a short distance.

21.7 Left onto County Highway C. The Village Inn on this corner serves up a good hot lunch.

32.5 Enter Chequamegon National Forest. This road follows the course of the Siskiwit River.

33.0 Right into Mount Valhalla Recreation Area, which has rest rooms and picnic tables. Backtrack to County Highway C.

33.3 Right onto County Highway C, which becomes Eighth Avenue in Washburn.
Residents of this spunky little city at the mouth of Chequamegon Bay rarely miss a chance to rib friends in Bayfield about how they stole the county seat in 1892. The long-standing grudge goes back to Washburn's heyday as a lumber town, when mills hummed around the clock, turning out more than 100 million board feet a year. The town is named for Cadwallader Washburn, Wisconsin's governor from 1872 to 1874.

41.7 Left onto WI 13 (West Bayfield Street).

42.1 Karlyn's Pottery Shop features pottery and paintings by local artists.

42.4 The 1890 bank to your left is built of local Potsdam sandstone, often called brownstone.
A high demand for the stone, used in courthouses, schools, and fashionable row houses in cities like Chicago, St. Louis, and New York, spurred the expansion of the

Pleasure boats in Bayfield Harbor

stonecutting industry in the 1880s and 1890s. A narrow belt of sandstone extends for about 8 miles along Chequamegon Bay and the south shore of Lake Superior to Port Wing. There are also extensive sandstone deposits on several of the Apostle Islands.

The stone varies in color and texture, though the local variety is usually reddish. It is a desirable building material because it maintains its color, disintegrates slowly, and hardens with time. At the turn of the 20th century, quarries near Washburn shipped out trainloads of the rock to major cities all over the country. Sandstone was rarely used in this area except for civic buildings. Examples in Washburn include this bank and the business block across the street.

43.0 Washburn City Park and Campground.
A picnic area and campground overlook Lake Superior and Madeline Island. Washrooms are available.

46.2 On your right is a historical marker, along with a view of Madeline Island in the distance.

51.3 The road to your left leads to Mount Ashwabay Ski Area.
This is the site of Lake Superior Big Top Chautauqua (715-373-5851). The Big Top features top-notch entertainment, from bards to banjo pickers, nearly every night during the summer months. Performers include homegrown talent and nationally known acts.

54.0 Smoked whitefish and trout are available at the Fish Market.

54.1 Left onto South Sixth Avenue in Bayfield.

54.4 Right onto Rittenhouse Avenue.

54.5 Old Rittenhouse Inn (715-779-5111) at the junction with Third Street.
This elegant Queen Anne–style mansion was built in 1890 by Allen Fuller, adjutant general for Illinois during the Civil War. Fuller vacationed in Bayfield, where he found relief from his bouts with asthma. The steeply pitched roof with prominent gables, enormous wraparound porch, and bay windows are characteristic of this turn-of-the-20th-century style.

In 1974, the home was purchased by Jerry and Mary Phillips, who have developed it into one of the Midwest's premier bed-and-breakfast inns. Guest rooms are lavishly decorated with antiques and working fireplaces. Whether or not you stay at the Old Rittenhouse Inn, dinner there is a Bayfield must-do. Dining room staff recite an ever-changing verbal menu with theatrical flair, an inn tradition that began when printed menus failed to arrive in time for opening day. The menus always incorporate fresh, local ingredients.

54.7 The corner of Rittenhouse Avenue and First Street—your starting point. *A local benefactor has provided Bayfield with an Olympic-size indoor swimming pool that is open to the public. Soak out the stiffness in the whirlpool or swim a few laps after your ride. The pool is located downtown, on the corner of Broad Street and Wilson Avenue. Call 715-779-3201 for current hours.*

For good food and a lively atmosphere, try Maggie's (715-779-5641) on Manypenny Avenue. Another personal favorite is Greunke's First Street Inn (715-779-5480), which offers quaint lodging and a nightly fish boil featuring Lake Superior whitefish; their other specialty is deep-fried whitefish livers, a local delicacy. Bayfield is the only place on the lake where commercial fishermen take the time to save the livers.

Bicycle Repair and Rental Service

Bay City Cycles, 412 Main Street West, Ashland; 715-682-2091

Trek & Trail, 7 Washington Avenue, Bayfield; 715-779-3595 or 1-800-354-8735 (rentals only)

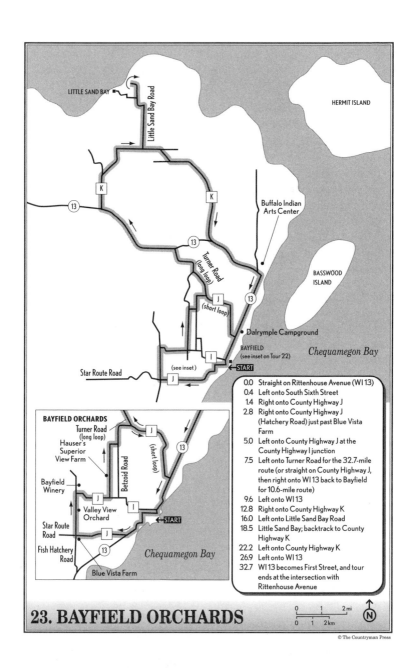

LITTLE SAND BAY

HERMIT ISLAND

Little Sand Bay Road

K

13

K

13

Buffalo Indian
Arts Center

BASSWOOD
ISLAND

Turner Road
(long loop)

J
(short loop)

13

Dalrymple Campground

J

BAYFIELD
(see inset on Tour 22)

Chequamegon Bay

←START

Star Route Road

(see inset)

J

BAYFIELD ORCHARDS

Turner Road
(long loop)

Hauser's
Superior
View Farm

J

Betzoid Road

(short loop)

J

13

Bayfield
Winery

J

Valley View
Orchard

I

←START

Star Route
Road

J

Fish Hatchery
Road

13

Chequamegon Bay

Blue Vista Farm

0.0	Straight on Rittenhouse Avenue (WI 13)
0.4	Left onto South Sixth Street
1.4	Right onto County Highway J
2.8	Right onto County Highway J (Hatchery Road) just past Blue Vista Farm
5.0	Left onto County Highway J at the County Highway I junction
7.5	Left onto Turner Road for the 32.7-mile route (or straight on County Highway J, then right onto WI 13 back to Bayfield for 10.6-mile route)
9.6	Left onto WI 13
12.8	Right onto County Highway K
16.0	Left onto Little Sand Bay Road
18.5	Little Sand Bay; backtrack to County Highway K
22.2	Left onto County Highway K
26.9	Left onto WI 13
32.7	WI 13 becomes First Street, and tour ends at the intersection with Rittenhouse Avenue

23. BAYFIELD ORCHARDS

0   1   2 mi
0   1   2 km

N

Bayfield Orchards

- **DISTANCE:** 10.6 or 32.7 miles
- **TERRAIN:** Rolling to hilly

This short spin takes you through the heart of Bayfield's fruit-growing area, where every month of the cycling season offers something fresh and juicy to pluck from the tree or vine. Strawberries ripen in late June or early July; followed by raspberries and blueberries in mid-July, cherries in early August, apples throughout September, and pears later in September. Because Bayfield is located on a peninsula, a "lake effect" moderates the temperature and results in a longer growing season than that of farms farther inland.

Cider flows freely at the Bayfield Apple Festival, celebrated during the first weekend of October for more than 30 years. This community event extraordinaire includes a parade, street fair, apple-peeling and pie-baking contests, and, of course, the coronation of the Apple Queen. It's worth planning a trip around the festival since the dates usually correspond perfectly with the peak of autumn color. Contact the Bayfield Chamber of Commerce (715-779-3335) for lodging suggestions.

This route follows paved (though occasionally rough) roads. Be prepared for a number of long, steep hills with sensational views of Bayfield and the Apostle Islands from the summits.

Follow WI 13 north to Bayfield, and begin at the corner of Rittenhouse Avenue (WI 13) and First Street, next to the Bayfield Inn.

The Bayfield Apple Festival is the first weekend in October.

0.0 Straight on Rittenhouse Avenue (WI 13).

0.4 Left onto South Sixth Street.

0.9 Eckels Pot Shop.
This well-known shop sells pottery made by several generations of the Eckels family.

1.4 Right onto County Highway J.

2.8 Right onto County Highway J (Hatchery Road) where Star Route goes straight, just past Blue Vista Farm.
The ski runs of Mount Ashwabay Ski Area are visible off to the left.

3.7 A detour down this road leads to Valley View Orchard, Organic Strawberry Farm, and North Wind Orchard.

5.0 Left onto County Highway J at the County Highway I junction.

5.6 Hauser's Superior View Farm and Bayfield Winery are on the left.
Stop for a moment and admire the far-reaching vista and sample the hard cider, mead, and country wines. The farm sells perennial plants by mail order.

7.5 Left onto Turner Road, if you plan to do the 32.7-mile route.
If you plan to do the 10.6-mile loop, continue straight on County Highway J and fol-
low it for 2 miles. Then turn right onto WI 13, which will take you back to your start-
ing point in Bayfield.

9.6 Left onto WI 13.

12.8 Right onto County Highway K.

16.0 Left onto Little Sand Bay Road.

18.5 Little Sand Bay. Backtrack to County Highway K.
Along the waterfront, with a commemorative plaque, you will find the hatch cover
of the Sevona, *a 373-foot steamer that was shipwrecked in Julian Bay, off Stock-*
ton Island, in 1905. Scuba divers and snorkelers still explore the wreck. The dock
here is the jumping-off point for the Inner Island Shuttle, which delivers backpack-
ers to some of the lesser-visited Apostle Islands.

Get a close-up view of the commercial fishing industry in the Apostles region
on a tour of Hokenson Brothers Fishery. Here Eskel, Leo, and Roy Hokenson ran a
successful fishing operation for more than 35 years until they retired in the 1960s.
Sons of Swedish immigrants, they came to the area to farm but turned to fishing
when farming didn't pay the bills. The tour, led by a National Park Service guide,
takes in the twine shed, where nets were constructed, mended, and stored; the ice
house, where ice cut from the lake during the winter months was kept; a dock with
a herring shed, where fish were cleaned, salted, and packed for market; and the
fishing tug Twilite, *used by the Hokensons for herring fishing.*

Scandinavian immigrants brought their fishing skills to the Bayfield area in the
late 1800s. During this period, fishermen abandoned sailing vessels in favor of
larger boats with steam engines, and fishing companies organized individual
fishermen into a single enterprise. Company boats made daily pickups from
fishing camps located among the Apostle Islands. The Bodin and Booth fisheries
were two of the largest operations, together employing more than 500 people.

The fishing industry still exists in Bayfield, and many restaurants serve a fresh
"catch of the day." But as time goes on, fewer and fewer people are willing to put in
the long hours required for mending nets and maintaining equipment, with no cer-
tainty that their efforts will pay off.

Whitefish, lake trout, and herring have always been the mainstays of the fishing
industry here. The abundance of each has varied through the years, and each has
at one time been the most lucrative catch. Fish populations were greatly reduced in

the 1950s and 1960s because of overfishing and the destructive sea lamprey (an eel-like creature that invaded the Great Lakes through the St. Lawrence Seaway), but lamprey control measures and restocking programs have restored most species.

22.2 Left onto County Highway K.

26.9 Left onto WI 13.

28.9 To your left is the Buffalo Indian Arts Center.
The center offers contemporary art displays, artifacts, and a gift shop selling Native American–made items. Across the road is the newly built Isle Vista Casino, which offers blackjack and slot machine gaming. A bingo hall is adjacent to the casino.

30.3 The Jam Factory sells homemade jams and jellies, a thriving cottage industry here.

31.6 Dalrymple Park Campground (715-779-5712) is to your left.
This 30-site facility with a prime location on the Lake Superior shore is operated by the city of Bayfield.

32.7 WI 13 becomes First Street.
The tour ends at the intersection with Rittenhouse Avenue, in front of the Bayfield Inn.

Bicycle Repair and Rental Service

Bay City Cycles, 412 Main Street West, Ashland; 715-682-2091

Trek & Trail, 7 Washington Avenue, Bayfield; 715-779-3595 (rentals only)

24

Madeline Island

- **DISTANCE:** 18.9 or 31.7 miles
- **TERRAIN:** Flat

Madeline Island might be called Wisconsin with a French accent. Roadsides lined with nodding lupines and tiger lilies seem born of the impressionist's brush, and a flotilla of sailboats whose boldly painted hulls bear names like *Esprit* and *Joie d'Vivre* bobs in the harbor. A longtime association with France has given the island a Gallic flair that is easier felt than defined.

Just a 20-minute ferry ride from the Bayfield peninsula, Madeline Island packs more history per square mile than any other corner of the state. The Chippewas called it *Monignwana Neisha,* meaning "home of the golden-breasted woodpecker," for the many flickers that nested near Grant's Point. The current name was bestowed in 1793 when Michel Cadotte, a fur trader for the North West Company, married Equaysayway, daughter of Chief White Crane, a Chippewa leader. Cadotte's bride was baptized at the time of their marriage and given the Christian name Madeleine. The island was named in her honor, though the spelling has changed slightly through the years.

There are now about 150 year-round residents on Madeline Island, a mere fraction of its population during the height of the Chippewa reign, when 13,000 Native Americans struggled to survive here. In the winter, residents and high school students travel to the peninsula across the ice on a plowed ice road. When the ice

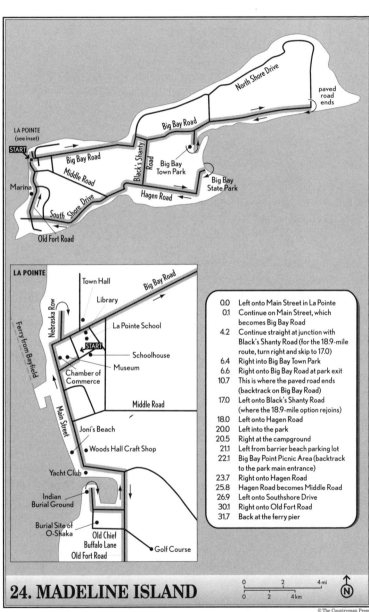

LA POINTE
(see inset)
START

North Shore Drive

paved
road
ends

Big Bay Road

Black's Shanty Road

Big Bay Road

Big Bay
Town Park

Big Bay
State Park

Middle Road

Marina

Hagen Road

South Shore Drive

Old Fort Road

LA POINTE

Town Hall

Library

Big Bay Road

Nebraska Row

La Pointe School

Ferry from Bayfield

START

Schoolhouse

Chamber of
Commerce

Museum

Middle Road

Main Street

Joni's Beach

Woods Hall Craft Shop

Yacht Club

Indian
Burial Ground

Burial Site of
O-Shaka

Old Chief
Buffalo Lane

Golf Course

Old Fort Road

0.0	Left onto Main Street in La Pointe
0.1	Continue on Main Street, which becomes Big Bay Road
4.2	Continue straight at junction with Black's Shanty Road (for the 18.9-mile route, turn right and skip to 17.0)
6.4	Right into Big Bay Town Park
6.6	Right onto Big Bay Road at park exit
10.7	This is where the paved road ends (backtrack on Big Bay Road)
17.0	Left onto Black's Shanty Road (where the 18.9-mile option rejoins)
18.0	Left onto Hagen Road
20.0	Left into the park
20.5	Right at the campground
21.1	Left from barrier beach parking lot
22.1	Big Bay Point Picnic Area (backtrack to the park main entrance)
23.7	Right onto Hagen Road
25.8	Hagen Road becomes Middle Road
26.9	Left onto Southshore Drive
30.1	Right onto Old Fort Road
31.7	Back at the ferry pier

24. MADELINE ISLAND

0   2   4 mi

0   2   4 km

N

begins to thaw in the spring, an engine-driven windsled, similar to an Everglades airboat, is used to make the crossing.

Madeline Island's past was molded by fur traders and missionaries. The first Europeans to tread on the island were the French explorers Radisson and Groseilliers (jokingly referred to as "Radishes and Gooseberries" in some old journals) in 1638. They were followed by Fathers Allouez and Marquette, who attempted to convert the Chippewas to Christianity in the 1660s and 1670s. The "black robes" eventually left with little success.

In 1693, Pierre Le Sueur took over as commander with a trading post near Grant's Point, launching the island into the lucrative fur trade. Furs were so abundant that in just three short years, Le Sueur glutted the market and Louis XIV cancelled all fur trade licenses. By 1717 the fur market had recovered and a new Frenchman, Louis Denis Sieur de la Ronde, took over. On his heels came Michel Cadotte, credited with establishing the first permanent settlement on the island near the present Old Fort Road. The fur boom continued well into the 1800s, when beaver pelts were in great demand because the animal's soft underhairs could be compressed into the stiff fabric used in fashionable top hats.

Boats operated by the Madeline Island Ferry Line (715-747-2051) leave from the pier at the west end of Front Street in Bayfield at least once an hour during the summer months. A visit to the island can be a leisurely full-day trip if you stop to savor all the sights or a half-day excursion if you don't linger too long. All of the roads included in this route are paved, and the terrain is absolutely flat. There are several casual restaurants in the village of La Pointe near the ferry pier.

If you find yourself waiting a while for the next ferry, check out the Cooperage Museum, located adjacent to the ferry pier parking area. This building once housed the Booth Fishery, which salted and packed fish in handmade barrels for shipment to market. On weekends you can see two coopers at work, assembling barrels over an open hearth. At one time, five coopers turned out 50,000 to 75,000 barrels a year. Refrigerated transportation, new packing methods, and the decline of the fishing industry led to the closing of the facility in the 1950s. The Cooperage includes a museum (no charge) and gift shop. Trek and Trail, which offers bicycle and kayak rentals, is also located in the Cooperage building.

0.0 When you arrive on Madeline Island, turn left onto Main Street in the village of La Pointe, or proceed straight ahead if you wish to begin with a side trip to the Madeline Island Historical Museum.
A 20-minute multimedia show called "Spirit of the Island" is shown in the Capser Center, which was added to the museum in 1991. Fast-paced, with a lively, locally composed score, the show takes you through three centuries of life on the island. Exhibits in the new wing of the museum include examples of European and Indian trade goods. The older wing, built in 1955 on the site of the American Fur Company building, includes some rare specimens of Native American clothing, beadwork, and tools. There is also a nice gift shop.

If you chose to visit the museum, you will need to backtrack to Main Street. Continue on Main Street, which becomes Big Bay Road (also County Highway H) as it makes a sharp right turn.

Straight ahead, as you turn, is a short dead-end street called Nebraska Row. This stretch of vacation homes is named for Colonel Frederick Woods of Lincoln, Nebraska. After renting a small cottage on the island, Woods broadcast the summer appeal of this spot and convinced many well-to-do families to build homes here. Among them was Hunter Gary, the founder of General Telephone, who, along with Woods, hosted Calvin Coolidge on his 1928 visit.

0.1 Continue on Main Street, which becomes Big Bay Road.

0.2 The Town Hall to your left was built in 1909 for $2,000.
The public library to your right is housed in an old school, dating to 1872. The present La Pointe grade school is just behind it.

4.2 For the 31.7-mile route, continue straight at the junction with Black's Shanty Road. Follow the signs toward Big Bay Town Park.
For the 18.9-mile route, turn right onto Black's Shanty Road. Pick up directions from mile 17.0.

6.4 Right into Big Bay Town Park, operated by the village of La Pointe.

6.5 A wooden footbridge crosses a lagoon, leading to the beach.
When Madeline Island reappeared from under the Wisconsin Glacier about 15,000 years ago, this lagoon was a large, shallow, open bay. Shoreline currents

Commercial fishing boats moored in Bayfield Harbor

and waves built the barrier beach that now separates the lagoon from the lake. There are rest rooms and a picnic area at the park.

6.6 Right onto Big Bay Road as you exit the park.
There are beautiful views as you ride along the Lake Superior shoreline.

10.7 This is where the paved road ends. Backtrack on Big Bay Road.

17.0 Left onto Black's Shanty Road toward Big Bay State Park.
This is where the 18.9-mile option rejoins the main route.

18.0 Left onto Hagen Road toward Big Bay State Park, Wisconsin's northern-most state park.

20.0 Left into the park and follow the road to Barrier Beach.

20.5 Right at the campground and follow signs to the picnic areas and Barrier Beach.

21.0 This 1½-mile-long strand is a beachcomber's delight.
There are rest rooms here.

21.1 Left from Barrier Beach parking lot and follow the road to Big Bay Point.

22.1 Big Bay Point Picnic Area.
Park your bike and follow the path to the Lake Superior shoreline. There are sandstone bluffs and caves at the water's edge.

   Backtrack to the park main entrance.

23.7 Right onto Hagen Road at the park exit.

25.8 Hagen Road becomes Middle Road. Continue straight here.

26.9 Left onto Southshore Drive.

30.1 Right onto Old Fort Road.

30.8 Here you will find the Old Indian Cemetery, established in 1836.
Notice the miniature houses that are used as grave covers to protect the dead, as well as the food left with the dead for nourishment on their four-day journey to the afterlife. A very weathered gravestone marks the burial spot of Chief Great Buffalo, a principal chief in the Great Lakes area, who signed the treaty creating Wisconsin's reservations in 1854. You will also find the grave of Michel Cadotte and his Chippewa wife, Madeleine. Chief Great Buffalo's son, O-Shaka, is buried in the clearing to your left as you leave the cemetery, between two pines marked with a colorful banner.

   These days, most people come to this end of the island for the Robert Trent Jones golf course and the upscale Clubhouse Restaurant, which has an excellent reputation.

31.2 Enter the village of La Pointe.

31.4 The La Pointe Public Park and Joni's Beach, to your left, has picnic tables and rest rooms.
The Woods Hall Craft Shop to your right features local arts and crafts.

31.7 You're back at the ferry pier.

Bicycle Repair and Rental Service

Bay City Cycles, 412 Main Street West, Ashland; 715-682-2091

Trek & Trail, 7 Washington Avenue, Bayfield; 715-779-3595 (rentals only)

WESTERN
WISCONSIN

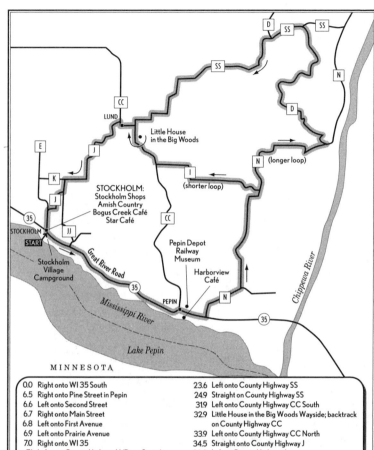

Little House
in the Big Woods

STOCKHOLM:
Stockholm Shops
Amish Country
Bogus Creek Café
Star Café

(shorter loop)

(longer loop)

STOCKHOLM
START

Stockholm
Village
Campground

Great River Road

Pepin Depot
Railway
Museum

Harborview
Café

Mississippi River

PEPIN

Lake Pepin

MINNESOTA

0.0	Right onto WI 35 South
6.5	Right onto Pine Street in Pepin
6.6	Left onto Second Street
6.7	Right onto Main Street
6.8	Left onto First Avenue
6.9	Left onto Prairie Avenue
7.0	Right onto WI 35
7.1	Left onto County Highway N (Dunn Street). Veer left by the Evangelical Free Church where County Highway N is called Pepin Hill Road

40.4-mile Option

12.8	Continue straight on County Highway N
14.9	Stay right on County Highway N
16.7	Left onto County Highway D

23.6	Left onto County Highway SS
24.9	Straight on County Highway SS
31.9	Left onto County Highway CC South
32.9	Little House in the Big Woods Wayside; backtrack on County Highway CC
33.9	Left onto County Highway CC North
34.5	Straight onto County Highway J
38.0	Left on County Highway J
38.5	Right on County Highway J
40.4	Cross WI 35 to reach your starting point at the campground

25.3-mile Option

12.8	Left onto County Highway I for 4.4 miles, then right onto County Highway CC
17.2	Rejoin the longer route at Little House in the Big Woods Wayside (skip to mile 32.9)

25. LAKE PEPIN/STOCKHOLM/ GREAT RIVER ROAD

Lake Pepin/Stockholm/ Great River Road

- **DISTANCE:** 25.3 or 40.4 miles
- **TERRAIN:** Rolling to hilly

One of Lake Pepin's most ardent admirers was William Cullen Bryant, who said its shores "ought to be visited in the summer by every painter and poet in the land." Bryant's suggestion was pure prophesy. The 1970s marked a wave of artistic immigration, as students of the Minneapolis Institute of Art, attracted by the wild beauty of the lake and its surrounding valleys, began to move into the area. Many have settled into drafty old farmhouses, converting them into studios as time and money allow.

The tiny crossroads village of Stockholm, where the tour begins, hosts an annual art fair on the third Saturday of July. The rest of the year, local artwork is available for sale at several small galleries. Amish-made goods, including quilts and hickory furniture, are sold at Amish Country. For nourishment, try the Bogus Creek Café and Deli, which serves healthy breakfasts and lunches on a sunny patio. Homemade baked goods are also available to carry out. The Star Café promises meals made from locally grown meats, vegetables, and berries. You'll see a variety of herbs and lettuces growing in the garden out back.

The oldest Swedish settlement in western Wisconsin, Stockholm was founded in 1851 by Eric Peterson and a group of immigrants from Kalskoga, Sweden. In the summer of 1939, Crown Prince Gustav of Sweden and his family visited the village. This

Bluffs along the Mississippi River provide challenging cycling.

fact is mentioned prominently in all of the town's promotional literature—a clue that nothing quite as exciting has happened since. Once a thriving community, Stockholm couldn't keep up with towns on the Minnesota side of the river and now claims only 104 residents. Stop in at the Stockholm Institute and Museum, a historical preservation society located in the old post office, for more information about Stockholm's past.

While there are no hotels in Stockholm at the present time, lodging is available in nearby towns. For a room with a view, try the Harrisburg Inn Bed and Breakfast (715-448-4500), a charming inn perched on the bluffs overlooking Lake Pepin. It's located in Maiden Rock, about 6 miles north of Stockholm on WI 35.

The tour begins at the Stockholm Village Campground, just off WI 35, on the shore of Lake Pepin. Simple campsites, rest rooms, parking, and water are available here. (Light sleepers should note the campground's proximity to the train tracks.) Mileage for the tour begins as you turn onto WI 35 after leaving the campground.

0.0 Right onto WI 35 South. There is moderate traffic, but the road has a generous shoulder.
If you brake for garage sales, expect to make slow progress. They are ubiquitous on this stretch, where nearly every home has a few tables out front.

2.3 A scenic overlook and historic marker here indicate the site of Fort St. Antoine, built by Nicholas Perrot to establish French sovereignty over the region.
A ceremony on May 8, 1869 officially informed both the Indians and the English that Perrot had claimed the entire region west of the Great Lakes, "no matter how remote," in the name of Louis XIV.
      Continue on WI 35.

5.1 Lake Pepin Wayside.
Lake Pepin is formed where the fast-moving waters of the Chippewa flow into the Mississippi, causing a backup of the sand and gravel carried down from Wisconsin farmlands. Named for Pepin le Bref, a French king, the lake is a boater's paradise, dotted with billowing spinnakers on a breezy day. It's not surprising that this alluring body of water inspired 18-year-old Ralph Samuelson to strap a set of boards on his feet and skim across its surface, inventing the popular sport of waterskiing here in 1922.
      A variety of products has been harvested from Lake Pepin and adjacent stretches of river through the years. River carp were seined from the lake and sold to kosher markets on the East Coast; freshwater clams were collected and the shells sold to button factories in Lake City, Minnesota; and commercial fishing continues to provide many with their livelihood. Clamming has made a comeback in the last 20 years, though these days clamshells are ground into pellets and sold to Japan for use in culturing pearls. The pellets are inserted into saltwater clams to begin pearl formation.

5.9 Enter the village of Pepin.

6.3 Pepin Depot Railway Museum and Laura Ingalls Wilder Historic Marker are to the left.
The depot includes a ticket office that looks much as it did a century ago. There is more information about Wilder at her birthplace later in the ride. A picnic area, water, and rest rooms are also available.

6.5 Right onto Pine Street toward the Pepin business district.

6.6 Left onto Second Street through downtown.

6.7 Right onto Main Street (past A Summer Place B&B) to the marina and the Harbor View Café.
Twin Cities sailors tie up outside for dinner at this popular waterfront restaurant. There's nearly always a wait of an hour or more for a Californiaesque menu of innovative salads, pastas, and fine wines. Take a stroll through town, watch the sunset over Wisconsin's "west coast," or browse through the stacks in the library-cum-waiting area. For burgers or a pizza, head for the Pickle Factory just across the way at the end of the pier.

6.8 Left onto First Avenue at the waterfront.

6.9 Left onto Prairie Avenue and up the hill.

7.0 Right onto WI 35.

7.1 Left onto County Highway N (Dunn Street). The last 0.7 mile is quite steep. At the hilltop, veer left by the Evangelical Free Church. County Highway N is called Pepin Hill Road at this intersection.

40.4-MILE OPTION

12.8 Continue straight on County Highway N.
For directions to the 25.3-mile option, see below.

14.9 Stay right on County Highway N at the intersection with Boyd Spring Road.

16.7 Left onto County Highway D.

23.6 Left onto County Highway SS.

24.9 Straight on County Highway SS where County Highway D goes right.

31.9 Left onto County Highway CC South.

32.9 Little House in the Big Woods Wayside is to your left. The shorter loop rejoins here. Turn right (backtrack) on County Highway CC at the Wayside exit.
Author Laura Ingalls Wilder, whose books have endeared her to several generations, was born on this spot in 1867. The log cabin is a replica of the one on which

Wilder based her childhood memories of the Pepin area in Little House in the Big Woods. *This was the first book in the* Little House *series, which Wilder began writing at age 65. Wilder's family moved to Kansas (her inspiration for* Little House on the Prairie*) but later returned to Pepin.*

33.9 Left onto County Highway CC North.

34.4 Enter the village of Lund.
The Little House Store sells Laura Ingalls Wilder souvenirs, as well as sodas and snacks.

34.5 Straight onto County Highway J where County Highway CC goes right.

38.0 Left on County Highway J where County Highway K goes straight at Sabylund Cemetery.

38.5 Right on County Highway J where County Highway JJ goes straight.

40.4 Cross WI 35 in Stockholm to your starting point at the campground.

25.3-MILE OPTION

12.8 Left onto County Highway I. Follow County Highway I for 4.4 miles, then right onto County Highway CC. This will take you to the Little House in the Big Woods Wayside on your right. Skip to the 32.9-mile mark for the remainder of the route.

17.2 Rejoin the longer route at Little House in the Big Woods Wayside (skip to mile 32.9).

Bicycle Repair Service

Four Seasons Bike Shop, 2311 West Main Street, Red Wing, MN; 651-385-8614

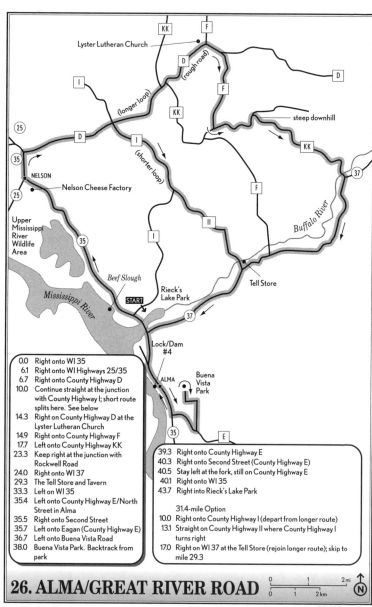

Lyster Lutheran Church

KK   F

D
(rough road)

F

I

(longer loop)

KK

steep downhill

25

D

I

KK

35

(shorter loop)

37

NELSON

Nelson Cheese Factory

25

F

Upper
Mississippi
River
Wildlife
Area

35

II

Buffalo River

I

Beef Slough

Mississippi River

START

Rieck's
Lake Park

Tell Store

37

Lock/Dam
#4

ALMA

Buena
Vista
Park

35

E

0.0	Right onto WI 35
6.1	Right onto WI Highways 25/35
6.7	Right onto County Highway D
10.0	Continue straight at the junction with County Highway I; short route splits here. See below
14.3	Right on County Highway D at the Lyster Lutheran Church
14.9	Right onto County Highway F
17.7	Left onto County Highway KK
23.3	Keep right at the junction with Rockwell Road
24.0	Right onto WI 37
29.3	The Tell Store and Tavern
33.3	Left on WI 35
35.4	Left onto County Highway E/North Street in Alma
35.5	Right onto Second Street
35.7	Left onto Eagan (County Highway E)
36.7	Left onto Buena Vista Road
38.0	Buena Vista Park. Backtrack from park

39.3	Right onto County Highway E
40.3	Right onto Second Street (County Highway E)
40.5	Stay left at the fork, still on County Highway E
40.1	Right onto WI 35
43.7	Right into Rieck's Lake Park

31.4-mile Option

10.0	Right onto County Highway I (depart from longer route)
13.1	Straight on County Highway II where County Highway I turns right
17.0	Right on WI 37 at the Tell Store (rejoin longer route); skip to mile 29.3

26. ALMA/GREAT RIVER ROAD

0   1   2 mi
0   1   2 km

N

© The Countryman Press

Alma/Great River Road

- **DISTANCE:** 31.4 or 43.7 miles
- **TERRAIN:** Gently rolling to hilly

If you're a romantic who can't resist the shrill whistle of a train or the throaty horn of a heavily laden barge, you'll feel right at home in this part of Wisconsin. Short of hopping a freight or signing on as an oarsman, bicycling is the best way to explore the scenery and history of the Upper Mississippi River Valley. Tourism dollars have just begun to reach this area, so you won't find trendy cafés, slick brochures, or fudge shops. Instead, the tiny river towns seem to be covered with a fine layer of silt, giving them the hue and charm of a sepia print. The landscape here is a medley of the mellow, gently rolling Great River Road and the challenging climbs of the "coulee country," steep, winding valleys where water flows only in the spring.

Squeezed between the river below and the bluffs above, Alma, the starting point of this tour, is 7 miles long and just two streets wide. There are so many turn-of-the-20th-century frame and brick houses that the entire town is on the National Register of Historic Places. Among the historic structures is the Italianate Laue House (608-685-4923) at 1111 South Main Street (WI 35). This is a laid-back bed-and-breakfast inn where you may find a note telling you to settle in to the room of your choice and help yourself to the player piano in the parlor. More upscale is the Gallery House B&B (608-685-4975) at 215 North Main Street, tucked away on the airy second floor of a brick mercantile building. Enjoy live entertainment at breakfast and browse through a watercolor and photography gallery on the street level.

Though named for a river town in Russia, Alma was originally settled by Swiss and German immigrants who followed the Mississippi north from Dubuque with plans to cut and sell cordwood to passing steamboats. One of the town's unique attractions is a fishing float in the river that rents tackle, sells bait, and serves up a hearty breakfast to early-bird anglers. To get to the float, walk to the end of Alma's municipal pier and wave your arms wildly—someone will come by with a boat to pick you up.

Take WI 35 to the tour starting point at Rieck's Lake Park (Alma Rod and Gun Club), just a few miles north of Alma at the junction with WI 37. Parking, rest rooms, water, showers, and a picnic shelter are available. People gather here in late autumn to watch the migration of rare tundra swans.

0.0 Right onto WI 35 and follow the river north, passing through the Upper Mississippi Wildlife Refuge.

The refuge, which includes 194,000 acres of bottomland from Wabasha, Minnesota, to Rock Island, Illinois, was established by the U.S. Department of Interior, Fish and Wildlife Service in 1924. This area was set aside for the perpetuation of migratory birds, native wildlife, and fishes.

About a mile north of Alma, you will pass Beef Slough, a sluggish branch of the Chippewa River. This was an excellent storage pond for logs being floated downstream from northern logging camps on the Chippewa, Eau Claire, and St. Croix Rivers. Each log was marked to identify its logger and the sawmill to which it was destined. The person charged with marking had to determine which side of the log would float upward and mark that side. Logs were laid side by side until enough were collected to make a 50- by 500-foot raft, called a brail. Four to six brails were chained together to form an even larger raft, which a steamboat pushed to a sawmill downriver. At its height, Beef Slough was the largest log sorting and rafting works in the world.

A conflict between the Eau Claire and Beef Slough Lumber Companies over where logs were to be sold (here or farther south) led to the Beef Slough War of 1868. Lumber baron Frederic Weyerhauser ended the dispute by turning Wisconsin's logging industry into an interstate industry.

Spinning down Great River Road

5.5 Enter the village of Nelson.
Old-timers remember when Nelson wasn't on the river at all—that was before the lock-and-dam system flooded the area now known as Nelson Bottoms, a huge section of backwater adjoining the Mississippi River, with thousands of acres of woods and abundant wildlife. Nelson is also popular with hang-gliding enthusiasts who soar off the high cliff behind town.

5.8 Castleberg Park has rest rooms and picnic tables.

5.9 Nelson Cheese Factory.
This fifth-generation cheese-making operation, begun by Hubert Greenheck in the mid-1850s, offers huge double-dip ice cream cones at bargain prices, as well as assorted cheeses.

6.1 Right onto WI Highways 25/35 through town.

6.7 Right onto County Highway D.

10.0 At the junction with County Highway I, the 43.7-mile route continues

straight on County Highway D where you will enjoy a nice downhill and see several picturesque round barns.
For the shorter 31.4-mile route, skip to the directions below.

12.4 Pass the first junction with County Highway KK and continue straight on County Highway D.
The road surface is rough for the next 2 miles, but this stretch offers some spectacular views.

14.3 Right on County Highway D at the Lyster Lutheran Church.
There is a picnic shelter here.

14.9 Right onto County Highway F.

17.7 Left onto County Highway KK at the hilltop.

19.0 A long downhill stretch starts here.
Ride in control and watch for loose gravel on the turns.

23.3 Keep right at the junction with Rockwell Road.

24.0 Right onto WI 37 just after crossing the Buffalo River.

29.3 The Tell Store and Tavern has rest rooms and sells snacks.
The shorter option rejoins the route here.

33.3 Left on WI 35 and continue into the village of Alma.

34.9 United States Government Lock and Dam #4 in downtown Alma.
Here you can watch riverboats, barges, and pleasure craft passing through the locks from an observation platform. Barges heading upstream are often carrying coal from the coal fields of southern Illinois and western Kentucky. Those heading downstream typically carry corn, oats, wheat, barley, and rye grown in Minnesota and Wisconsin. Diesel towboats guide as many as 12 to 15 barges at a time, totaling 20,000 tons of freight.

35.4 Left onto County Highway E/North Street in Alma.

35.5 Right onto Second Street.

35.7 Left onto Eagan (County Highway E) and begin the ascent to Buena Vista.

36.7 Left onto Buena Vista Road.
The last mile of the climb after this turn is very steep. Even if your knees demand you walk this stretch, it's well worth it for the view from the top. We promise!

38.0 Buena Vista Park.
Looking over Alma's shoulder from a towering bluff 500 feet above town, the park offers an awesome view of the Mississippi River and the Minnesota shore.

39.3 Right onto County Highway E as you exit the park.
Enjoy the downhill!

40.3 Right onto Second Street (County Highway E).

40.5 Stay left at the fork, still on County Highway E.

40.1 Right onto WI 35.

43.7 Right into Rieck's Lake Park.

31.4-MILE OPTION

10.0 Right onto County Highway I.

13.1 Straight on County Highway II where County Highway I turns right.

17.0 Right on WI 37 at the Tell Store.
The shorter route rejoins the longer route here. Refer to the 29.3-mile mark above.

Bicycle Repair Service

Bikes LTD, 1001 La Crosse Street, La Crosse; 608-785-2326
Valley Ski & Bike, 321 Main Street, La Crosse; 608-782-5500

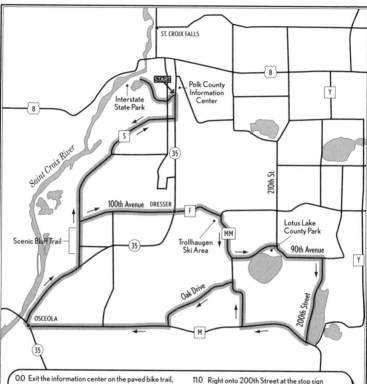

0.0	Exit the information center on the paved bike trail, cross WI 35
0.4	Continue straight on WI 35, where the bike trail turns right into Interstate State Park
1.2	Right onto County Highway S (River Road)
4.4	Left onto 100th Avenue, which becomes State Street
6.7	Cross WI 35 and continue straight on County Highway F
7.8	Right onto County Highway MM at the Trollhaugen Ski Area
8.8	Left onto 90th Avenue
9.3	Lotus Lake County Park
9.9	Right onto 210th Street, which becomes 90th Avenue after a 90-degree turn
11.0	Right onto 200th Street at the stop sign
12.9	Right onto County Highway M
14.5	Right onto County Highway MM at the hilltop
15.6	Left onto Oak Drive
17.6	Right onto County Highway M, which becomes Seminole Avenue in Osceola
20.6	Right onto Cascade Street (WI 35)
22.4	Left onto County Highway S across from the high school
27.0	Left onto WI 35
27.8	Left into Interstate State Park (continue on loop and then backtrack on the park road)
33.2	Left onto the bike trail that parallels WI 35
33.6	The Polk County Information Center

27. ST. CROIX FALLS/ INTERSTATE STATE PARK

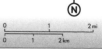

St. Croix Falls/
Interstate State Park

- **DISTANCE:** 33.6 miles
- **TERRAIN:** Rolling to hilly

What could have become a border battle ended with an act of brotherly affection when Wisconsin and Minnesota agreed to create Interstate State Park, the first park in the country to span two adjacent states. The park encompasses the Dalles of the St. Croix River, a magnificent gorge with 220-foot rock cliffs that entice rock climbers as well as more terrestrial tourists.

The focal point of this ride is the St. Croix River, a nationally recognized Scenic Riverway, which forms part of the Wisconsin-Minnesota border. The river, characterized by stretches of fast water and falls, was created by the melting Wisconsin Glacier. Lake Superior, known as Glacial Lake Duluth by geologists, was so full of water and silt that it began to overflow its banks. The force and volume of this water created the St. Croix River and the Dalles you will see as you cycle through the Wisconsin side of Interstate State Park.

Plan to stop for lunch or a snack in the river towns of St. Croix Falls and Osceola. One bit of advice—don't spend too long searching for the falls in St. Croix Falls. The town's namesake, a spectacular series of rapids that fell 40 feet in 6 miles, was buried underwater by the construction of a dam and hydroelectric power plant in the early 1900s. There is a scenic overlook in the downtown area that faces the site of the falls and the power facility.

Opposite this is the historic Festival Theatre (715-483-3387), a professional theater company housed in an old-time vaudeville hall that is undergoing extensive restoration.

Nearby Osceola has its own waterfall to boast about. An exploring party stumbled upon Cascade Falls in the early 1800s and quickly staked a claim. This led to the founding of Osceola and the establishment of a gristmill on the site. The remnants of the old mill are across from the city park. A 156-step stairway leads you down to the base of the falls, where you can swim on a hot day. An equally pleasant option is to watch the swimmers and enjoy a fruit smoothie on the back deck of the Coffee Connection restaurant.

There are a number of bed-and-breakfast inns in the area. One of the more unusual is the Wissahickon Farms Country Inn, which offers accommodations in a cabin that replicates a frontier general store. The inn, located on a 30-acre hobby farm, offers bicycle repair services and adjoins the Gandy Dancer bicycle trail. If someone in your group prefers pampering to pedaling, Majestic Falls (715-483-3175), an Aveda spa and retreat, is located just north of St. Croix Falls on WI Highway 87.

This tour begins at the Polk County Information Center on the outskirts of St. Croix Falls. To get there, take US Highway 8 from the east or west to St. Croix Falls. Then exit on MN State Highway 35 South. The information center is on your left, just south of Highway 8.

This is also the starting point for the Gandy Dancer Trail, a 50-mile crushed limestone trail along an abandoned railroad bed from St. Croix Falls to Danbury. The trail's name comes from the railroad workers who used tools made by the Gandy Tool Company. These workers became known as Gandy Dancers. While not included as part of this tour, the trail is well worth riding if you have the time.

The friendly staff at the information center can help with information about the area, maps, and trail passes for the Gandy Dancer Trail. There are rest rooms inside and a large parking lot. The mileage for the tour starts where the bike trail meets the parking lot, next to the two black mailboxes.

Most roads have little traffic other than a stray Holstein.

0.0 Exit the information center on the paved bike trail, toward WI 35. Cross WI 35 with caution and continue straight on the trail.

0.4 Continue straight on WI 35, where the bike trail turns right into Interstate State Park.
We'll visit the park later.

1.2 Right onto County Highway S (River Road).

4.4 Left onto 100th Avenue (careful, this is easy to miss), which becomes State Street in the village of Dresser.

6.7 Cross WI 35 and continue straight on County Highway F.
Dresser Junction Railway Station is on the left. This is the old stopping point of the St. Croix–to–Osceola Railway Line. There are picnic tables here.

7.8 Right onto County Highway MM at the Trollhaugen Ski Area.

8.8 Left onto 90th Avenue.

9.3 Lotus Lake County Park.
Picnic tables, rest rooms, and water are available. Continue on 90th Avenue.

9.9 Right onto 210th Street.
After a 90-degree turn, 210th Street becomes 90th Avenue.

11.0 Right onto 200th Street at the stop sign.
This is a scenic ride along the shoreline of Horse Lake.

12.9 Right onto County Highway M where 200th Street ends.

14.5 Right onto County Highway MM at the hilltop.

15.6 Left onto Oak Drive.

17.6 Right onto County Highway M and follow it to the village of Osceola.

20.0 Enter the village of Osceola. County Highway M becomes Seminole Avenue.

20.6 Right onto Cascade Street (WI 35) in Osceola.

20.9 Downtown Osceola.
The Coffee Connection, with a view of Cascade Falls, is on your left as you enter downtown. The St. Croix River Inn (715-294-4248) is a historic bed and breakfast located on River Street overlooking the St. Croix River.
    Continue north on WI 35 through the village of Osceola.

22.4 Left onto County Highway S across from the high school.

23.4 The parking area for the Scenic Bluff Trail is on the left.
It is worth the short walk to the bluff overlooking the St. Croix River.

27.0 Left onto WI 35. This is a busy road with an ample shoulder.

27.8 Left into Interstate State Park.
This is a beautiful 5-mile loop, but quite challenging. If you don't wish to make the descent and ascent, ride back to the visitors center and drive to the park.

28.2 Pass the ranger station. You don't need to pay admission when bicycling.

28.3 The visitors center and gift shop.
There is a short video about the history of the park along with geological displays. Ride in control as you descend to the river. About halfway down the hill is a scenic lookout over the Dalles.

29.3 Lake O' the Dalles Beach parking area.
Rest rooms, water, picnic tables, and a swimming beach are available. Exit the parking area and continue toward the river. Keep right throughout the loop.

30.3 Boat landing and trailhead for the Bluff Trail.
There are picnic shelters and rest rooms here, as well as a nice river beach. A short hike leads up the bluff trail for a magnificent view of the Dalles. You might also catch a glimpse of a restored paddle-wheel boat that does tours through the Dalles, leaving from Taylors Falls on the Minnesota side of the river. Call 651-465-6315 for tour information.

Continue on the loop around the picnic area and then backtrack on the park road. This is a steep ascent!

33.2 Left onto the bike trail that parallels WI 35.

33.6 The Polk County Information Center.
If you continue on WI 35 under the bridge you will come to the historic downtown of St. Croix Falls. The information center has a walking tour map. There are also shops and restaurants.

Bicycle Repair Service

Wissahickon Farms Country Inn, 2263 Maple Drive, St. Croix Falls; 715-483-3986

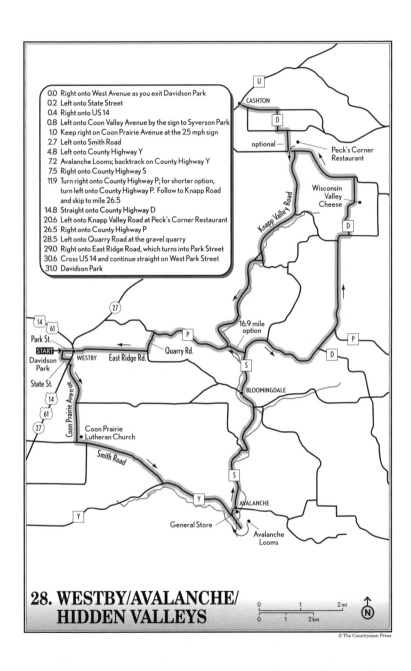

0.0 Right onto West Avenue as you exit Davidson Park
0.2 Left onto State Street
0.4 Right onto US 14
0.8 Left onto Coon Valley Avenue by the sign to Syverson Park
1.0 Keep right on Coon Prairie Avenue at the 25 mph sign
2.7 Left onto Smith Road
4.8 Left onto County Highway Y
7.2 Avalanche Looms; backtrack on County Highway Y
7.5 Right onto County Highway S
11.9 Turn right onto County Highway P; for shorter option,
     turn left onto County Highway P. Follow to Knapp Road
     and skip to mile 26.5
14.8 Straight onto County Highway D
20.6 Left onto Knapp Valley Road at Peck's Corner Restaurant
26.5 Right onto County Highway P
28.5 Left onto Quarry Road at the gravel quarry
29.0 Right onto East Ridge Road, which turns into Park Street
30.6 Cross US 14 and continue straight on West Park Street
31.0 Davidson Park

28. WESTBY/AVALANCHE/
HIDDEN VALLEYS

0   1   2 mi
0   1   2 km

N

© The Countryman Press

Westby/Avalanche/ Hidden Valleys

- **DISTANCE:** 16.9 or 31 miles
- **TERRAIN:** Rolling to hilly

The spirit of "Velkommen" lives on today in Westby and the surrounding communities. Norwegian settlers began arriving in southwestern Wisconsin in the mid-1800s to what they called "Norskedalen" (the Norwegian Valley). They were attracted by the terrain of this unglaciated region, which reminded them of their homeland. Also, they felt at home with the long Wisconsin winters. In Westby, the "Stabbur" tourist information center is a replica of a Norwegian barn. The Norskedalen Nature and Heritage Center is open from June 1 to August 31. It is a short distance away in the village of Coon Valley.

Norwegian heritage is celebrated with food and festivals throughout the year in the village of Westby. "Sytende Mai" in May commemorates Norway's independence from Sweden. It features a parade and a giant quilt auction sponsored by the Norwegian and Amish communities. Each January, athletes from around the world compete in Norway's national sport, ski jumping, at the Olympic-sized ski jump just outside of Westby. The annual Lutefisk and Meatball dinner takes place in February. For a hearty pre-ride breakfast, you can sample the Norwegian pancakes with lingonberries at Borgen's Café and Bakery. You may also want to stock up on snacks from the Westby Bakery and Coffee Shop. Their lefsa, cookies, and pastries can help you with the quick energy you will need later.

As you cycle out of Westby, don't be surprised to see a grouping of horse-drawn carriages at the local hitching post and carriage barn. The Amish began settling northeast of Westby in the late 1970s. This is now the largest Amish community in Wisconsin. In the fields, men plant and harvest with combines pulled by draft horses. Women can be seen hanging clothes to dry in the wind and tending the beautiful flower gardens outside their homes. The Amish are also known for their bentwood hickory furniture, hand-made quilts, jams and maple syrup, and baked goods. Hand-hewn signs will lead you to the farms where these goods are for sale. All are closed on Sundays. The Amish are kindred spirits with cyclists in their mode of travel. They will share a wave and smile as they pass in their buggies, but most prefer not to have their picture taken.

Both the longer and shorter options of this tour will first explore the winding roads and hidden valleys of this region. The cycling through the valleys and along the creek beds is flat to rolling. The end of the 16.9-mile ride includes a long gradual uphill climb back into Westby. On the longer option, there are some challenging climbs and breathtaking descents as you travel through the Amish country. This tour begins in the village of Westby at Davidson Park. Take WI 14 to Westby from the east or west. Go south on Park Drive for two blocks to Davidson Park. There is ample parking along with rest rooms, a picnic shelter, and water.

0.0 Right onto West Avenue as you exit Davidson Park.

0.2 Left onto State Street.

0.3 The Westby House Restaurant and Victorian Inn (608-634-4112). *The Westby House offers lodging and gourmet breakfasts and dinners. Next to the inn is the Westby Pharmacy and Soda Fountain. Stop on your way back for a soda or sundae.*

0.4 Right onto US 14. Pass through downtown Westby.

0.6 The Westby Cooperative Creamery has a showroom for the many cheeses they produce. They ship throughout the country.

Winding through the valleys of coulee country

0.8 Left onto Coon Valley Avenue by the sign pointing to Syverson Park.

1.0 Keep right on Coon Prairie Avenue at the 25 mph sign.

2.2 Continue straight on Coon Prairie Avenue at the Country Coon Prairie Lutheran Church.
This was the first of many Lutheran churches in the area and where the first settlement of Westby was located.

2.7 Left onto Smith Road.

4.8 Left onto County Highway Y and follow it to Avalanche.

6.8 Enter Avalanche.

7.0 The Avalanche General Store. Stop in for snacks, drinks, or other provisions.
The Avalanche General Store is in the original one-room school building. At its peak, Avalanche boasted a cooperage factory, a feed and flourmill, a spool-carding and knitting mill, wagon and blacksmith shop, and a buggy factory.

7.1 Go straight toward Avalanche Looms where County Highway Y makes a sharp right turn.
If you follow County Highway Y for 2 more miles, you will come to the Pietsch Tree Farm Bed and Breakfast (608-634-3845). Lodging is in a restored log cabin.

7.2 Avalanche Looms.
Designer/weaver Susan Johnson incorporates the surrounding nature into her weaving. Prairie grasses like the native blue stem are woven into the wall hangings and table runners. The chenille scarves have the pattern of the wooly bear caterpillars. Watch the weaving on one of the antique Norwegian looms. There is also a small gift shop with cards and crafts.

Backtrack on County Highway Y from Avalanche Looms to the Avalanche General Store.

7.5 Right onto County Highway S.
This is a beautiful winding road that follows the West Fork of the Kickapoo River, a favorite with fly-fishermen.

10.9 Enter the village of Bloomingdale.
The old Bloomingdale School has a picnic shelter.

11.9 For shorter option, turn left onto County Highway P. Follow to Knapp Road and skip to mile 26.5.
There is a challenging climb as you ascend out of the valley and a series of roller coaster hills as you ride along the ridge tops.

14.8 Straight onto County Highway D where County Highway P turns right.

18.3 Old Country Cheese Store.
Take a break to view cheese being made and sample some of the squeaky cheese curds. Rest rooms are available.

20.6 Left onto Knapp Valley Road at Peck's Corner Restaurant.
If you want to add 5 miles to the route, you can ride into the village of Cashton. Follow County Highway D to WI 33. Turn left onto WI 33 and follow it into town. There are a several small shops and eateries. Backtrack to Peck's Restaurant and turn right onto Knapp Valley Road.

26.5 Right onto County Highway P. (The short and long routes merge here.)

28.5 Left onto Quarry Road at the gravel quarry.

29.0 Right onto East Ridge Road, which turns into Park Street as you enter Westby.

30.6 Cross US 14 and continue straight on West Park Street.

31.0 Davidson Park.

16.9-MILE OPTION

11.9 Turn left onto County Highway P and follow it until you reach WI 27.

16.5 Join the long option at mile 26.5 above.

Bicycle Repair Service

Bikes LTD, 1001 La Crosse Street, La Crosse; 608-785-2326

Valley Ski & Bike, 321 Main Street, La Crosse; 608-782-5500

RAILS-TO-TRAILS
SAMPLER

29

Favorite Railroad-Bed Trails

Biking on railroad-bed trails offers several advantages: you can ride two abreast and chat as you bike; you don't need to keep checking your map or directions; the terrain is nearly flat; and there's no traffic noise or worry. Trails also provide a fun, safe outing for small children who are beginning bikers.

Since a list of bicycle trails is included in the *Wisconsin Biking Guide* available from the Wisconsin Department of Tourism (see *Resources* in Introduction) and because all of the trails are easy-to-follow, point-to-point routes, we haven't detailed them in this book. There is a trail fee to ride most of the trails. Currently it is $5 daily or $20 for the season. The season pass is quite a bargain, as you can use this pass on all state trails.

We think all of the trails are worth riding in their entirety, but a few stretches stand out as our favorites.

A. MILITARY RIDGE TRAIL
Verona to Riley, 14.2 miles round-trip

Start the tour at the trailhead on County Highway PB just south of WI 18/151 in Verona. Take a Sunday morning spin along the watershed of the Sugar River, ending up at the itty-bitty burg of Riley, where in-the-know cyclists congregate for blueberry pancakes at the Riley Tavern. The tavern (restaurant would be more appropriate as this is a family-style event) occupies what was once a general store and post office when "Riley's Station" was a water stop on the steam engine line between Madison and Lancaster. Stoke up on a stack of cakes, and reverse your course to the starting point.

B. SUGAR RIVER TRAIL

New Glarus to Albany, 32 miles round-trip

New Glarus is a picturesque small town founded in the 1840s by immigrants from the canton of Glarus, Switzerland. Swiss heritage remains strong, with a summer schedule chock-full of Swiss cultural events. Begin at the trail headquarters, a century-old Milwaukee Road depot, and follow the trail to Albany. If you don't have the energy for a round-trip, you can arrange for someone to drop you off along the trail and drive your car back to the start. The trail follows the Sugar River watershed through pleasant farmland and prairie land. End the ride with dinner at the New Glarus Hotel—schnitzel, weissbeer, and old-world ambience.

Bicycle Repair Service

Dan Atkin's Bicycle Shoppe, 517 Half Mile Road, Verona; 608-845-6644

C. GLACIAL DRUMLIN TRAIL

Cottage Grove to Lake Mills, 31.4 miles round-trip with optional extension to Aztalan State Park

Start at the trailhead located on County Highway N just south of Interstate 94 in Cottage Grove. The trail heads east to Lake Mills, where several downtown cafés serve hearty stick-to-your-ribs food. If you want to divide the ride into a two-day trip, the Bayberry Inn (414-648-3654) offers bed-and-breakfast accommodations; more elegant lodging is available at the Fargo Mansion Inn (414-648-3645). Continue on the trail past Lake Mills to County Highway Q, turning left to Aztalan State Park. Aztalan, the most important archaeological site in Wisconsin, has been called "America's Stonehenge." You can climb giant mounds, built by Native Americans between A.D. 1100 and 1300, which served as a solar calendar. It's also possible to return to Cottage Grove on County Highway BB, which parallels the trail.

Bicycle Repair Service

Village Pedaler, 5511 Monona Drive, Monona; 608-221-0311

D. GREAT RIVER TRAIL

Trempealeau to northern end of trail, 17 miles round-trip

Park near the Trempealeau Hotel, a historic riverside restaurant/hostelry that serves good vegetarian and nonvegetarian food in a serene setting overlooking the mighty Mississippi. There's often live music on an outdoor stage during the summer. The trail begins a few blocks away—ask for directions at the hotel. The highlight of this trip is Perrot State Park, where a short hike to Brady's Bluff provides a spectacular view of the converging Trempealeau and Mississippi Rivers. Beyond the park, the trail borders the Trempealeau National Wildlife Refuge, passing bottomlands where herons, egrets, and ospreys are frequently seen.

Bicycle Repair Service

Bikes LTD, 1001 La Crosse Street, La Crosse; 608-785-2326

Valley Ski & Bike, 321 Main Street, La Crosse; 608-782-5500

E. RED CEDAR TRAIL

Menomonie to Downsville, 15 miles round-trip

Park at the trail headquarters just off WI 25 in Menomonie. This scenery-packed trail clings to the course of the Red Cedar River, with pleasant pullouts along the way. Downsville thrived in the late 1800s when Knapp, Stout, and Company was the largest white-pine milling company in the world. The company store still stands on the north side of Main Street; the original hotel is across the street. One block east of the store is the Empire in Pine Museum, which brings to life the colorful lumbering era. A little farther down Main Street is the Creamery Inn and Restaurant, a

222 RAILS-TO-TRAILS SAMPLER

delightful place for a "civilized" lunch—fettucine with smoked salmon and herbal iced tea, for instance—served on a screened porch overlooking the river valley. If you are looking for a longer ride, this trail now connects with the Chippewa River State Trail. This 23-mile hard-surfaced trail follows the scenic Chippewa River toward the city of Eau Claire.

Bicycle Repair Service

Red Cedar Outfitters, 910 Hudson Road, Menomonie; 715-235-5431

Spoke House Cyclery, 632 South Broadway, Menomonie; 715-235-1440

F. BEARSKIN TRAIL

Minocqua to the South Blue Lake Rest Area, 20 miles round-trip

The trail begins on WI 51 in downtown Minocqua. The Bearskin Trail offers a true wilderness experience, passing through the Northern Highland/American Legion State Forest and past dozens of pristine lakes. Because of the expense of shipping limestone screenings to northern Wisconsin, crushed granite was used as a trail surface on the Bearskin. Look for loons as you pass Baker Lake and evidence of beavers at work farther along. The trail leaves the railroad grade and travels on old Baker Lake Road for a short stretch. Pick up the makings for a picnic in Hazelhurst, a short detour off the trail; enjoy your lunch on the shores of South Blue Lake, which has a park with a picnic area and rest rooms. On the return, work up an appetite for an all-you-can-eat family-style feast at Paul Bunyan's on WI 51 in Minocqua.

Bicycle Repair Service

BJ's Sport Shop, 917 WI 51 North, Minocqua; 715-356-3900

G. ELROY-SPARTA TRAIL

Elroy to Sparta, 32 miles

It's worth riding every mile of this trail. Developed in 1966, the Elroy-Sparta was the country's first rails-to-trails conversion. The

Author Scott Hall on the 32-mile Elroy-Sparta Trail

trail offers a raised vantage point overlooking verdant farmland, along with three tunnels ranging from ¼ to ¾ mile in length. The tunnels are cool, moist, and very dark, so bring a jacket and a flashlight. If you stay at the Tunnel Trail Campground (608-435-6829) near the midpoint at Wilton, you can bike to opposite ends on two days. Wilton is also where you want to be when the Lions Club serves up a pancake breakfast in the municipal park every Sunday morning, June to September. If you wish to bike the entire trail in one day, a car shuttle service is available from the trail headquarters in Kendall.

The Elroy-Sparta Trail draws more than 60,000 visitors a year. There's plenty of camaraderie on weekends, but it's surprisingly peaceful during the week or slightly off-season.

The Elroy-Sparta Trail is now connected to three other trails: The 400 Trail, La Crosse River Trail, and the Great River Trail. If you could leave a car at either end, you could make a Century Ride from Reedsburg to Perrot State Park.

Bicycle Repair Service

Speed's Bike Shop, 1126 John Street, Sparta; 608-269-2315

H. THE BOULDER AREA TRAIL SYSTEM-CRYSTAL LAKE TRAIL

22 miles round-trip

Although not officially a rails trail, this newly paved trail starts just south of Boulder Junction. It meanders 11 miles through the Northern Highlands/American Legion State Forest under a canopy of tall white and red pine trees. Be sure to pack a lunch and a swimming suit as you will pass three state forest picnic and swimming areas: North Trout Lake, South Trout Lake, and Crystal Lake. This trail will make a nice combination for a two-day trip to the North Woods with our Boulder Junction/Manitowish Waters ride, chapter 19.

Bicycle Repair Service

Coontail Sports, 5466 Park Street, Boulder Junction; 715-385-0250